Eyes Open 3
WORKBOOK

Vicki Anderson with **Eoin Higgins**

CAMBRIDGE
UNIVERSITY PRESS

DISCOVERY
EDUCATION

Contents

Starter Unit

Meeting people

1 ★ Put the sentences in the correct order to make a conversation.

___ **Karen and Jackie:** See you later!
___ **Jackie:** Hi Pete. Nice to meet you.
___ **Pete:** Hello. I'm Pete.
_1_ **Karen:** This is my friend. Her name's Jackie.
___ **Pete:** You too. Well, I have to go.
___ **Pete:** Yes, bye!
___ **Karen:** Hi. My name's Karen. What's your name?

Routines

2 ★ Complete the daily activities. Use the words in the box. Then number the activities in the order you do them every day.

go (x2)   do   ~~wake~~   get   have (x3)

___ _____ lunch
___ _____ to bed
___ _____ up
___ _____ breakfast
_1_ __wake__ up
___ _____ to school
___ _____ homework
___ _____ dinner

Free-time activities

3 ★★ Write the activities under the pictures. Use *do*, *go*, *play*, *read*, *sing*, or *watch*.

play basketball

Wh- questions

4 ★ **Complete the questions with the words in the box.**

> What   Where   When   How
> How old   Who   Whose

1. **A:** _____How old_____ were you when you started playing tennis?
   B: I was 5 years old.
2. **A:** _____ did you go after school yesterday?
   B: I went to the swimming pool.
3. **A:** _____ is that girl over there?
   B: That's Giulia. She's Italian.
4. **A:** _____ are you doing?
   B: I'm sending a message to Oliver.
5. **A:** _____ phone number is this?
   B: It's Noah's. I have to call him later.
6. **A:** _____ did you go to Colombia?
   B: Last summer. It was great.
7. **A:** _____ do you switch on this tablet?
   B: It's easy. Press here.

Adjectives

5 ★ **Use the clues to complete the crossword.**

Across
4. makes you angry
7. strange
9. fantastic
10. makes you laugh

Down
1. makes you want to run away
2. someone that will help you
3. someone that doesn't like you
5. opposite of interesting
6. always smiling and positive
8. someone who cannot wait

Comparative and superlative adjectives

6 ★ **Circle the correct options.**

1. This film is much **more** / **most** frightening than that one.
2. What's the **easiest** / **easier** subject at school?
3. Many people think Real Madrid are **better** / **best** than all other football teams.
4. Playing a sport is much **more** / **most** exciting than watching one!
5. You can move **more fast** / **faster** in a city by motorbike than by car.
6. Dubai has got the **taller** / **tallest** building in the world.

Adverbs

7 ★ **Complete the sentences with the adverb form of the adjectives in brackets.**

1. I learned the song _____easily_____ (easy) because I had a good teacher.
2. Jack draws very _____ (good). He's a very good artist.
3. That app is difficult to use. Read the instructions _____ (careful).
4. They walked _____ (slow) on the beach in the evening sun.
5. My dad plays basketball _____ (bad). He can't get the ball into the basket!
6. I chatted _____ (happy) for an hour with my friend Lola last night.
7. We should talk _____ (quiet) because my little brother's asleep.
8. Grace did her homework _____ (quick) because she wanted to watch TV.

Comparative and superlative adverbs

8 ★★ **Write sentences with the comparative or superlative forms of the adverbs.**

1 Harry / learned / swim / easily / me
Harry learned to swim more easily than me.

2 The man / ran / quickly / the police
_____

3 They / played / the sad songs / quietly
_____

4 He / spoke / slowly / than / the first time
_____

5 My dad / drives / carefully / of all the family
_____

6 Lydia / writes / good / me
_____

Past simple

9 ★ ⟨Circle⟩ **the correct words in the table.**

1	In the past simple we add *-ed* or *-d* to the infinitive in **regular / irregular** verbs.
2	To form negatives, we put *didn't* + **infinitive / past form**.
3	To form questions, we put *Did* + subject + **infinitive / past form**.
4	We form negatives and questions of irregular verbs in **the same / a different** way.

10 ★★ **Complete the text. Use the past simple form of the verbs in brackets.**

Last year I ¹____had____ (have) a terrible experience when a shark ²_____ (attack) me. That day I ³_____ (not see) the red danger flag at the beach, so I ⁴_____ (decide) to go surfing. Suddenly I ⁵_____ (hear) someone shouting, and the next minute I ⁶_____ (see) the shark a few metres away from me. I ⁷_____ (jump) off my surfboard, the shark ⁸_____ (open) its mouth, and I ⁹_____ (hit) it hard on the nose. The surfboard ¹⁰_____ (break) in half. I don't know why, but the shark ¹¹_____ (not attack) me again. It ¹²_____ (swim) away very fast. How lucky!

11 ★★ **Write questions for a local politician. Use the prompts and the past simple.**

1 What problems / the town / have?
What problems did the town have?

2 So / you / build flood defences?
_____

3 What / you / do?
_____

4 How much / it / cost?
_____

5 Where / you / get the money?
_____

6 Why / people / start to call you a green town?
_____

12 ★★ **Complete the politician's answers. Use the verbs in the box in the past simple. Then match the answers (a–f) with the questions in Exercise 11.**

~~reach~~   decide   give   have   move
not think   be   not pay

a The total ¹_*reached*_ more than $6 million.
Question: _4_

b Because we ²_____ to put solar panels on all the new buildings. We ³_____ the first green town in the USA!
Question: ___

c We ⁴_____ terrible floods every two or three years because the town was by the river.
Question: ___

d No, the experts ⁵_____ that normal protection could stop the floods.
Question: ___

e The town ⁶_____ all the money. The government ⁷_____ us $4 million.
Question: ___

f The people of the town ⁸_____ all the houses and shops up the hill!
Question: ___

13 ★★ It is 8 o'clock in the evening. Look at the table and write sentences in the past simple about Dylan with *ago*.

8.00 am	12.00 pm	1.00 pm	5.00 pm	7.00 pm	7.55 pm
got up	had a Maths test	have lunch	go to the park	arrive home from judo class	wash his hands

1 *He got up twelve hours ago.* _____
2 _____
3 _____
4 _____
5 _____
6 _____

14 ★★ Answer the questions. Use *ago*.
1 When did you start school today?
   Three hours ago. _____
2 When did you last go on holiday?
   _____
3 When did you start to learn English?
   _____
4 When did you have breakfast today?
   _____
5 When did you last go to the park with your friends?
   _____

Explaining a problem

15 ★★ Match the sentences with the correct place in the conversation.

A: William, what's the matter?
B: ¹ *b*
A: Oh no! Your Maths homework?
B: ² ___
A: OK, don't panic! Where did you put it when you finished it?
B: ³ ___
A: But it's not in your bag. Is it in your Maths book?
B: ⁴ ___
A: Why not?
B: ⁵ ___
A: Well, where could it be, then?
B: ⁶ ___
A: I hope so!

a Let me think. In the classroom? It's probably in there.

b I lost my homework.

c I'm not sure. I think I put it in my bag.

d No way!

e Yes. It took me over an hour. I don't know what to do.

f Well, for one thing. Why would I put it in my Maths book?

① Extreme living

Vocabulary

Extreme weather

1 ★ Complete the crossword. Use the pictures.

							¹				
	²					³h	a	i	l		
			⁴								
⁵									⁶		
		⁷									
⁸											

Across

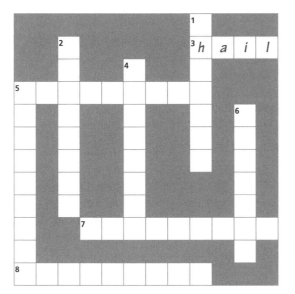

Down

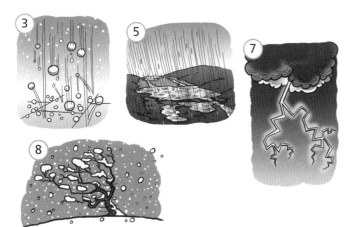

2 ★ Circle the odd one out.
1 boiling   heavy rain   freezing
2 heatwave   boiling   high winds
3 heavy rain   thunder and lightning   freezing
4 hail   snowstorm   boiling
5 freezing   heatwave   snowstorm

3 ★★ Complete the sentences with the correct form of the extreme weather words from Exercise 1.
1 Germany has a lot of ___hail___ storms. Sometimes the stones are like tennis balls. They're enormous!
2 Moscow is the city with the most _____ . It has 1,000 vehicles to remove snow!
3 In Helsinki there are 169 days below 0 °C. That's similar to Alaska! It's _____ .
4 In the summer months there are _____ in many cities, which can kill people!
5 Écija near Córdoba is the hottest place in Europe. It's _____ there in August!
6 Amsterdam, Paris and Rome airports are having problems with _____ of over 100 km per hour.

4 ★★ Complete the texts about the weather. Use the words in the box.

> rain   ~~snowstorms~~   hail   thunder
> freezing   lightning   winds

Many European countries are in chaos this morning because of heavy ¹ _snowstorms_ , high ² _____ and ³ _____ temperatures. In Poland the temperature is −26 °C.

NEWS ...

Two hours ago
There's a spectacular storm here! The heavy ⁴ _____ means we can't go out. We can see ⁵ _____ over the sea, and hear the ⁶ _____ . It's very loud. It's cold too and sometimes there's ⁷ _____ . It's really big – I hope it doesn't break anything! What's the weather like where you are? 👍 💬

5 ★★★ What's the weather like in spring, summer, autumn and winter in your country? Write sentences about the things in Exercise 1.

We don't have snowstorms here very often, but it's usually boiling in the summer.

Language focus 1

Present simple vs. present continuous

1 ⭐ **Choose the correct options.**

1 When it's freezing, we (don't go)/ aren't going out.

2 There's a snowstorm right now so we **stay** / **'re staying** at home.

3 I always **play** / **am playing** basketball on Saturdays.

4 The temperature **falls** / **is falling** each year in winter so there's a lot of snow.

5 I **learn** / **'m learning** German at the moment because I want to go to Germany in December.

6 It's 8 o'clock in the morning and I **have** / **'m having** breakfast.

2 ⭐ **Complete the sentences with the correct form of the present simple or present continuous. Use the verbs in the box.**

> not spend ~~come~~ look come
> go snow not go

1 It's November and winter ___is coming___ in Canada.

2 It's very cold and silent today. _____ it _____ outside?

3 The polar bear _____ for a place to hibernate in winter.

4 We _____ much time at the beach in the autumn. It's very cold.

5 _____ you _____ to visit us this year?

6 I _____ skating today because there's no ice, but I usually _____ on Sundays.

3 ⭐⭐ **Complete the mini-conversations. Use the present simple or the present continuous form of the verbs in brackets.**

1 **A:** What ___is Laura doing___ (Laura do) at the moment?

   B: She _____ (be) on holiday with her parents, I think.

2 **A:** What _____ usually _____ (you do) at the weekends?

   B: Not much, so I _____ (enjoy) this camping trip. It's great!

3 **A:** _____ (you make) a cake for the party?

   B: Yes, but we _____ (not know) what to do next! _____ (we do) it right?

4 ⭐⭐ **Complete the interview with a park ranger. Use the present simple or the present continuous form of the verbs in brackets.**

Interviewer: Today I ¹ _'m talking_ (talk) to Safri, who's a ranger at the Royal Belum State Park, Malaysia. Safri, what ² _____ a park ranger _____ (do)?

Safri: Well, we ³ _____ (protect) wild animals from hunters, and we ⁴ _____ (look) after the park. I ⁵ _____ (work) here this summer because the permanent rangers ⁶ _____ (not have) much free time to spend with visitors. All this week I ⁷ _____ (tell) visitors about our work here and I ⁸ _____ (show) them the animals. It ⁹ _____ (be) a great job!

5 ⭐⭐⭐ **Complete the email with the correct form of the present simple or present continuous. Use the verbs in the box.**

> have (x2) play ~~sit~~ rain do (x2)
> not go go run

✉ **New Message**	Send	Cancel

Hi Kim,
Well, here I am in Scotland! I ¹ _'m sitting_ in my room. It ² _____ again so people ³ _____ down the streets. There's another girl in my house called Carmen. She ⁴ _____ a shower right now. We ⁵ _____ out this afternoon. We usually ⁶ _____ two English classes in the morning and in the afternoon we ⁷ _____ our homework and ⁸ _____ sports. On Wednesdays, we often go swimming but I ⁹ _____ today because Carmen wants to go to the cinema. ¹⁰ _____ you _____ anything interesting? Write and tell me!
Eva

6 ⭐⭐⭐ **Choose a place and invent a special weekend. Imagine you are there. Write at least five sentences about it.**

I'm in Rome at the moment with .... We're sitting in ...

Listening and vocabulary

Survival essentials

1 ★ **Add vowels to the words to make travel essentials.**

> TRCH CMR ~~CNTCT LNSS~~ PNKNF
> SLPNG BG CMPSS MP WTR BTTL
> FRST D KT SNGLSSS SN CRM GLSSS

1 _contact lenses_	7 _____
2 _____	8 _____
3 _____	9 _____
4 _____	10 _____
5 _____	11 _____
6 _____	12 _____

2 ★★ **Complete the text with words for travel essentials from Exercise 1.**

We had a scary experience in the mountains last weekend. There was a landslide! And now I know why Dad always tells me to pack my bag carefully before we go walking. The ¹ _first aid kit_ was essential because a rock hit me. I didn't have a lot of water in my ² _____ but I cleaned the cut in the river. We couldn't continue our route because of the landslide, and it was very late so we stayed the night in the forest. It was very dark but we had the ³ _____ , and my ⁴ _____ was very warm. Another problem was that I didn't have the case for my ⁵ _____ , but I can't sleep in them so I put them in a plastic cup. For breakfast the next morning we only had some old bread and cheese. The bread was hard but I had my ⁶ _____ to cut it with. After that we used the ⁷ _____ and ⁸ _____ to find another way home and we finally arrived home after five hours, really tired!!

Listening

3 ★ 🔊 01 **Listen to the story of Laurie, a Canadian teenager, on a radio programme called 'Lucky escapes'. What did she escape from and how?**

4 ★★ 🔊 01 **Listen again and answer the questions.**

1 Where is Laurie from?
   She's from Canada.

2 When did the story happen?
   _____

3 Why was Laurie in the forest?
   _____

4 Why did they realise they were in danger?
   _____

5 What did they take with them?
   _____

6 Why did they start running?
   _____

7 How did they find the river?
   _____

8 How did they travel down the river?
   _____

9 Why was the torch useful?
   _____

10 How many hours were they in the river?
   _____

Language focus 2

Past simple vs. past continuous

1 ★ (Circle) the correct options.

1 They (cancelled) / were cancelling our flight because a volcano **erupted / was erupting** two days before in Iceland.

2 Where **did you go / were you going** when I **saw / was seeing** you in the street?

3 A police officer **stopped / was stopping** us from going into our house because there **was / was being** a big fire.

4 When the river water **rose / was rising** after the heavy rain, it **came / was coming** near the town centre.

5 While the rescue workers **looked / were looking** for people, they **found / were finding** a little boy.

6 The lights **came / were coming** on again while I **looked / was looking** for my torch.

7 I **cut / was cutting** my finger when I **used / was using** the penknife.

8 Ellie **fell / was falling** over while she **ran / was running** away from the fire.

2 ★★ Write sentences with the prompts.

1 When / I / watch TV / the lights / go out
When I was watching TV, the lights went out.

2 When / we / see the landslide / we / drive home
_____

3 She / ski / when / she / hear / the avalanche
_____

4 The rescue helicopter / arrive / when / the family / phone for help
_____

5 A fire fighter / give them / water / when / they / wait for an ambulance
_____

6 I / drink / from my water bottle / when / I / see / a helicopter
_____

3 ★★ (Circle) the correct options in the text.

In 2012 there was a serious earthquake in Guatemala. When it **¹(happened) / was happening**, fire fighter Tina Watson **² watched / was watching** TV at home in Los Angeles. But only two days later, she and Chester, her search and rescue dog, **³ flew / was flying** into Guatemala to help. On the first day, they **⁴ found / were finding** two survivors, but on the second day they **⁵ didn't find / weren't finding** any. Then, on the third day, Tina and Chester **⁶ searched / were searching** an apartment block, when they **⁷ located / were locating** three teenage girls trapped in the ruins. They were very thirsty, so Chester **⁸ took / was taking** them Tina's water bottle until more rescue workers **⁹ arrived / were arriving**. Amazingly, when they finally **¹⁰ pulled / were pulling** the girls out, they weren't injured.

4 ★★★ Write sentences that are true for you about five of the times in the box. Use the past simple or the past continuous.

> 25th December 2013   yesterday at 1 pm
> last August   this time last Saturday
> my last birthday   9 o'clock on Sunday morning

This time last Saturday I was watching a film with my friends.

(E)xplore prepositional phrases

5 ★★ Complete the sentences with the prepositional phrases in the box.

> on the planet   in both directions   on a ship
> on the island   ~~on the Internet~~

1 You shouldn't believe everything you read *on the Internet* .

2 The Antarctic is one of the coldest places _____ .

3 It's only four kilometres from the coast but nobody lives _____ .

4 We looked left and right but there was nothing but houses _____ .

5 There are no flights so you have to travel _____ to the island.

Reading

1 ★ **Read the text about Matt Suter. What unusual thing happened to him? How old was he?**

Matt Suter, from Missouri, USA, is lucky to be **alive**. In 2006 he became one of the few people to experience the inside of a tornado and survive.

Matt was a high-school student at the time and was relaxing at home in his grandmother's **trailer** when he heard a noise like a jet plane, which got louder and louder. One minute he realised that the walls and the floor of the trailer were moving, and the next minute all the windows and doors exploded. It was a tornado.

A lamp hit Matt on the head, and he **lost consciousness**. At that moment the tornado **sucked** him out of the trailer and he disappeared. When he woke up, he was lying in a **field** of soft grass, a long way from the trailer. His head was **bleeding** where the lamp hit him and his feet were cut, but surprisingly, that was all. A neighbour found him, and they went to look for his grandmother. Luckily, she also survived, under the ruins of the trailer.

The tornado carried 19-year-old Matt nearly 400 metres from the trailer and then dropped him. Now he **holds** a strange world **record**: he is the person to travel the longest distance in a tornado and survive! For a while he was a celebrity. He appeared on television to talk about his experience, but he didn't have very much to say because, unfortunately, he can't remember anything about what happened after the lamp **knocked** him **out**!

2 ★★ **Match the words in the box with the definitions. Use the words in *bold* in the text to help you.**

> field   alive   trailer   suck   bleed   ~~lose consciousness~~
> hold a record   knock (someone) out

1 go into an unconscious state (like sleep) _____ *lose consciousness*
2 the opposite of dead _____
3 a piece of farmland _____
4 a mobile home or caravan _____
5 lose blood in an accident _____
6 be the best person in the world at something _____
7 hit someone and make them unconscious _____
8 pull into your mouth _____

3 ★★ **Read the text again. Put the events in order.**
a Matt found his grandmother. ___
b The tornado lifted Matt and carried him away. ___
c He appeared on TV. ___
d Matt was relaxing in his grandmother's trailer. _1_
e Matt woke up in a field. ___
f A tornado hit the trailer. ___
g A lamp hit Matt on the head. ___

4 ★★ **Read the text again. Are these sentences true (*T*) or false (*F*)? Correct the false sentences.**
1 Matt Suter is from England. *F*
   Matt Suter is from the USA.
2 Matt was 19 when the tornado happened.
   _____
3 A plane hit the trailer where Matt was.
   _____
4 Matt landed on a road 400 metres from the trailer.
   _____
5 The lamp hit Matt after the tornado hit the trailer.
   _____
6 The police found Matt in a field.
   _____
7 His grandma didn't die in the tornado.
   _____
8 Matt told everyone how it felt to be in a tornado.
   _____

5 ★★★ **Imagine Matt is giving a TV interview. Write at least five questions and answers.**

Interviewer: How did it start?
Matt: Well … I was sitting in our trailer when I heard a loud noise.

Writing

An email to a friend

1 Read the email from Joe to his friend Ricky. What's the weather like on his holiday?

> ✉ *Your*MAIL ⊕ New Reply | ▼ Delete Junk | ▼
>
> Hi Ricky,
> Thanks ¹__*for*__ your ²_____ .
> It's ³_____ to ⁴_____ from you!
> We're having a fantastic holiday in Arizona! We're visiting national parks in a camper van. We cook all our meals in the van and we sleep in sleeping bags outdoors under the stars – with a torch of course. I love it! At the moment we're in the Petrified Forest National Park. There's a photo attached – isn't it amazing? There are lots of fossils from 225 million years ago! We love walking, but it's boiling during the day so we try to go early in the morning before the temperature rises. We always bring sun cream and water bottles.
> ⁵_____ are you doing at the ⁶_____ ?
> Are you enjoying your holidays?
> Write ⁷_____ soon,
> Best wishes,
> Joe

2 Complete the email from Joe to his friend Ricky. Use the words in the box. There are four extra words.

> moment ~~for~~ great what get
> soon email tell your back hear

Useful language Opening and closing an email ————

3 Read Joe's email again. How does he open and close the email?
Opening: ¹_____ Ricky,
Closing: ²_____ , ³_____

4 Complete the phrases for opening and closing an email with the words you didn't use in Exercise 2.
1 Write back and _____*tell*_____ me your news.
2 It was great to _____ your email.
3 Hope to hear from you _____ .
4 How are you and _____ family?

Writing

5 Put the words in order to make questions.

1 moment / are / What / doing / at / you / the?
What are you doing at the moment?

2 good time / you / Are / having / a?
_____

3 going / you / Where / holiday / on / are?
_____

4 do / day / you / What / do / the / during?
_____

5 you are / What's / where / the / like / weather?
_____

6 a / send / Can / photo / you / me?
_____

6 Complete the sentences with the correct prepositions of time.

1 We sleep in sleeping bags _____*at*_____ night.
2 We start walking _____ it gets too hot.
3 We're on holiday in Canada _____ the moment.
4 What do you do _____ the day?
5 There are a lot of things to do _____ the morning.

> **WRITING TIP**
>
> **Make it better!** ✓ ✓ ✓
> Use negative questions to ask the reader to agree with you and to show surprise.

7 Use the words to make negative questions.

1 photo / amazing
Isn't the photo amazing?

2 boiling / during the day?
_____

3 you / be / on holiday / yet?
_____

4 want / sleep under the stars?
_____

5 my new sunglasses / cool?
_____

6 the summer / great?
_____

8 Read the email again. Number the things in the list in the order they appear.

transport	___	weather	___
accommodation	___	activities	___
place in now	*1*	interesting facts	___

PLAN

9 Imagine you are on holiday in an exciting place. Use the headings in Exercise 8 and your imagination. Write notes.

WRITE

10 Write an email to a friend about your holiday. Look at page 17 of the Student's Book to help you.

_____
_____
_____
_____
_____
_____
_____
_____
_____
_____
_____
_____
_____
_____
_____
_____
_____

CHECK

11 Check your writing. Can you say YES to these questions?

- Is the information from Exercise 8 in your email?
- Have you got opening and closing phrases in your email?
- Are the prepositions of time correct?
- Do you use negative questions for surprise?
- Is the word order in the questions correct?
- Are the spelling and punctuation correct?

Do you need to write a second draft?

Vocabulary
Extreme weather

1 Match the words with the correct definitions.

1 hail
2 boiling
3 thunder
4 freezing
5 lightning
6 heavy rain

a very hot
b very wet weather
c very cold
d small pieces of ice
e flashes of electricity in the sky
f a loud crashing noise in a storm

Total: 5

Survival essentials

2 Complete the sentences with the words in the box.

> camera   torch   ~~compass~~   sunglasses
> penknife   map   sun cream
> contact lenses   water bottle
> sleeping bag

1 We'll have to use the ___compass___ to find the right direction.
2 Look at the _____ and that will help you plan your journey.
3 Take a _____ so you can see in the dark.
4 I've got a _____ so we can take pictures.
5 You should use _____ to protect your skin.
6 Do you use _____ to help you see better, or glasses?
7 I always carry a _____ to cut my food.
8 Don't forget your _____ to protect your eyes from the sun.
9 We'll take a _____ so that we are warm at night.
10 Have you got a _____ to carry something to drink?

Total: 9

Language focus
Present simple vs. present continuous

3 Complete the mini-conversations with the present simple or present continuous form of the verbs in brackets.

1 A: Is she doing her homework? (do homework)
  B: Yes, ___she is___ .
  A: _____ ? (always / do homework / in her bedroom)
  B: Yes, _____ .

2 A: What _____ ? (do)
  B: He _____ . (run a marathon)
  A: How often _____ ? (he / train)
  B: He _____ . (train / every day)

3 A: _____ ? (read a book)
  B: No, _____ .
  A: _____ ? (like reading)
  B: No, _____ .

Total: 10

Past simple vs. past continuous

4 Complete the text. Use the past simple or the past continuous form of the verbs in brackets.

NARROW ESCAPE for mountain hikers

A group of hikers ¹_____had_____ a close escape when they ²_____ (hike) in the mountains last Friday. 'At around midnight, I ³_____ (look) at the stars when suddenly I ⁴_____ (see) a bright light in the sky. I ⁵_____ (not know) what to do! The others ⁶_____ (sleep) in their tents so I woke them up and we all ⁷_____ (run) to our car and ⁸_____ (drive) away as fast as possible,' said Rob, one of the hikers. 'Fortunately, we ⁹_____ (escape)!'

Total: 8

Language builder

5 Complete the email with the missing words. (Circle) the correct options.

1	**a** have	**(b)** are having	**c** do have
2	**a** were sailing	**b** was sailing	**c** sailed
3	**a** see	**b** were seeing	**c** saw
4	**a** waked up	**b** were waking up	**c** woke up
5	**a** is	**b** did be	**c** was
6	**a** had	**b** have	**c** were having
7	**a** hardly ever erupts	**b** erupts hardly ever	**c** hardly erupts ever
8	**a** in the year	**b** in year	**c** a year
9	**a** take	**b** took	**c** 'm taking
10	**a** 'm wrote	**b** write	**c** wrote

Total: 9

✉ *Your* MAIL   ⊕ New   Reply | ▼   Delete

Dear Sue,

We ¹___ a wonderful time on our holiday in Oregon. Last weekend, we ²___ along the coast when we ³___ some whales. And yesterday morning, we ⁴___ to see a cloud of white smoke at the top of the mountain. It ⁵___ a volcanic eruption! They ⁶___ a really big eruption here a few years ago, but now the volcano ⁷___ – maybe once ⁸___ or less. I ⁹___ lots of photos of it! Don't forget I ¹⁰___ in my blog every day so you can read all my news there.

See you soon,

Julie

Vocabulary builder

6 (Circle) the correct options.

1 Are you ___ swimming now?
  a doing   **(b)** going   **c** playing

2 We can't go anywhere. There's a big ___ outside.
  a hail   **b** snowstorm   **c** rain

3 How many people live ___ the island?
  a in   **b** at   **c** on

4 We're laughing because this photo is very ___ .
  a funny   **b** scary   **c** bored

5 What time do you ___ breakfast?
  a go   **b** get   **c** have

6 We can play the football match ___ if it rains.
  a indoors   **b** in   **c** on the door

7 The sun is coming out and the temperature is ___ .
  a falling   **b** rising   **c** freezing

8 We'll take a ___ so that we can see at night.
  a penknife   **b** map   **c** torch

9 Use a ___ to find out which direction we are walking in.
  a torch   **b** compass   **c** kit

10 It's good for you to ___ exercise every day.
  a do   **b** play   **c** have

Total: 9

Speaking

7 (Circle) the correct phrase to complete each mini-conversation.

1 **A:** I think small schools are good because the teachers are friendly.
  B: (Perhaps you're right) / I don't think so. My school is small and the teachers are really friendly.

2 **A:** I think big schools are really noisy.
  B: I think / Maybe, but small schools are often noisy, too!

3 **A:** I reckon it's easier to make friends in a small school.
  B: I suppose so / I don't think so, but I think it's hard to make friends anywhere.

4 **A:** There's more variety of subjects in a big school.
  B: I don't think so. / Yes, that's true. I go to a small school and we can choose from over 20 different subjects.

5 **A:** The sports facilities are better in a big school.
  B: I reckon / I don't agree. A lot of big schools don't have good sports facilities.

Total: 4

Total: 54

Present simple vs. present continuous: *Wh-* questions

Remember that:
- we use the **present simple** to talk about facts, habits and routines
- we form *Wh-* questions in the **present simple** with *Wh-* + *do/does* + subject + infinitive without *to*. Remember to use *do*.
  - ✓ *Where do you go on Saturday mornings?*
  - ✗ ~~*Where you*~~ *go on Saturday mornings?*
- we use the **present continuous** to talk about actions in progress at the time of speaking
- we form *Wh-* questions in the **present continuous** with *Wh-* + *be* + subject + *-ing*. Remember to put *be* before the subject.
  - ✓ *What are you doing here today?*
  - ✗ *What are you doing here today?*

1 **Are the questions correct? Correct the incorrect questions.**

1 What you do when it's freezing outside?
   What do you do when it's freezing outside?

2 What do you do at the moment?
   _____

3 Who usually comes to your house at the weekend?
   _____

4 Where your cousin Michael lives?
   _____

5 What are you doing when it snows in your town?
   _____

6 How often you go to school by car?
   _____

7 What James is studying at the moment?
   _____

8 What does time school finishes?
   _____

Past simple vs. past continuous

Remember that:
- we use the **past continuous** (*was/were* + *-ing*) to talk about a long action that was in progress in the past
  - ✓ *Sam was jogging when he got lost.*
  - ✗ *Sam* ~~*jogged*~~ *when he got lost.*
- we use the **past simple** to talk about completed events and actions in the past.
  - ✓ *Then suddenly, he realised he was lost.*
  - ✗ *Then suddenly, he* ~~*was realising*~~ *he was lost.*

2 **Find and correct six more mistakes with the past simple and continuous in the email.**

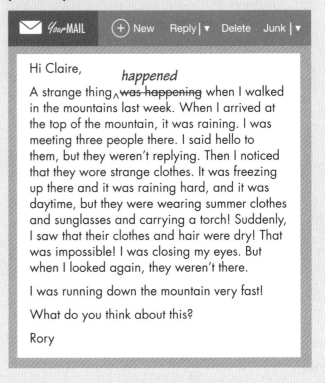

Hi Claire,

happened
A strange thing ∧ ~~was happening~~ when I walked in the mountains last week. When I arrived at the top of the mountain, it was raining. I was meeting three people there. I said hello to them, but they weren't replying. Then I noticed that they wore strange clothes. It was freezing up there and it was raining hard, and it was daytime, but they were wearing summer clothes and sunglasses and carrying a torch! Suddenly, I saw that their clothes and hair were dry! That was impossible! I was closing my eyes. But when I looked again, they weren't there.

I was running down the mountain very fast!

What do you think about this?

Rory

Prepositional phrases: time expressions

Remember that:
- we use *in* with months, seasons and years
  - ✓ *In June and July, the snow melts.*
  - ✓ *Who returned to the island in 1962?*
  - ✓ *My class goes on school trips in spring.*
- we use *on* with days of the week and phrases with days of the week
  - ✓ *We go to the cinema on Sundays.*
  - ✓ *We usually go shopping on Saturday morning.*
- with times of day when the day of the week is not mentioned, we use *in*
  - ✓ *It's difficult to see our friends in the evening.*

3 **Complete the sentences with *in* or *on*.**

1 We often go shopping _____*on*_____ Saturday afternoons.

2 _____ July it's usually boiling, but _____ October, we have heavy rain.

3 Are you coming out _____ Friday?

4 What are the average temperatures _____ winter?

5 It's 10.30 _____ the morning and it's sunny.

6 It's sunny and warm _____ spring.

2 A balancing act

Vocabulary

Priorities

1 ★ **Complete the word puzzle with the clues. What is the mystery word?**

1		s	p	o	r	t	s	
2								
3								
4								
5								
6								
7								
8								

1 My friend Matt loves doing ____*sports*____ . He plays football, volleyball and tennis.

2 I go to bed after midnight so I don't get enough _____ .

3 My Mum always says 'With work and family I never have _____ by myself'.

4 I spend a lot of time on the Internet chatting with my friends _____ .

5 My friend Alex draws comics. She loves doing _____ things.

6 Clara loves going to the shopping mall to _____ out with friends.

7 We're going to shop for _____ on Saturday.

8 Everyone helps _____ the house at the weekend. I hate it!

Mystery word: These are all activities that a _____ does.

2 ★ **Match the verbs with the nouns.**

1 competing in   **a** time by yourself
2 hang out   **b** around the house
3 doing   **c** something creative
4 getting   **d** enough sleep
5 having   **e** sports events
6 helping   **f** with friends

3 ★★ **Complete the text with words from Exercises 1 and 2.**

I come from a large family. It's not easy! We all take turns ¹*helping around the house* , like washing the floor or cleaning the bathroom. I usually get my older sisters' dresses and jeans when they're too small for them, so I can only dream about ² _____ .

We've only got two computers too, so we don't ³ _____ very often. Also, ⁴ _____ is difficult – there's always something happening with the family. And ⁵ _____ is a problem, because when we go to bed my sisters and I sometimes talk for hours!

Of course I don't always go out with my big sisters, I ⁶ _____ of my own from school. My sisters and I all enjoy painting and drawing, too. ⁷ _____ together is really nice. I also ⁸ _____ . I do athletics and it's great when all my family come to support me! We're all very close!

4 ★★★ **What about you? Write at least five sentences about your priorities. Use vocabulary from Exercises 1 and 2. Explain how you spend your time in the week and at the weekend.**

I don't help around the house in the week, but on Saturday I do.

Language focus 1

should/must

1 ★ **Complete the rules in the table.**

1	In the affirmative we use *should* + the _____ .
2	We form negatives with _____ after *should*.
3	We form questions with *should* _____ the subject.
4	We use *should* to say we think something is a _____ idea.

2 ★ **Complete the text with *should* or *shouldn't*.**

My brother and I share a room and we're always fighting. He always says I **1** ___should___ study more before my exams and I **2** _____ play computer games all the time. I tell him he **3** _____ leave his clothes on the floor, and that he **4** _____ go to bed earlier. Then he says I **5** _____ tell him what to do because he's older, and I say he **6** _____ have more respect. That's when Mum or Dad usually come in to say we **7** _____ stop shouting! **8** _____ we stop arguing all the time? I suppose so, but it's fun!

3 ★ (Circle) **the rules in the table.**

1	When we make the affirmative, negative and question with *must* and *should*, the grammar is **the same / different**.
2	We use the infinitive **with / without** *to* after *must* and *mustn't*.
3	We use *must* and *mustn't* to say we think something is **very / not** important.

4 ★★ **Complete the sentences with the correct form of *must* and the verbs in the box.**

remember ~~see~~ go help
tell stay get up watch

1 You ___must see___ these photos on my phone. They're great!
2 They _____ without us! Tell them to wait.
3 We _____ late on Saturday. We need to catch the bus at 9 o'clock.
4 _____ I _____ around the house now? I'm watching my favourite programme!
5 Joel _____ out late tonight. He's got an important match tomorrow.
6 Why _____ you _____ football all the time? I hate it!
7 You _____ me about your trip to Bogotá.
8 We _____ to text Jenny about the cinema.

5 ★★★ **Write sentences with *should/shouldn't* and *must/mustn't* and the words in brackets.**

1 It's very cold outside. (coat / catch)
  You should wear a coat or you'll catch a cold.
2 I'm sometimes tired in my Maths class. (get / more sleep)
  _____
3 I never remember what homework I have to do. (concentrate)
  _____
4 I've got a really important exam tomorrow. (go to bed / late)
  _____
5 I usually get very hungry before lunch. (snack)
  _____
6 Olivia really wants me to help her. (call / her later)
  _____

Explore verb + noun collocations

6 ★★ **Match the sentence halves.**

1 Why are you watching
2 I'm hungry! I think I'll
3 You must get
4 I think I'm catching
5 We can't concentrate
6 Tom loves surfing

a in our lesson because there's too much noise.
b TV? Go outside and play!
c the Internet but he should go out more.
d more sleep! You look very tired.
e a cold. I don't feel well.
f have a snack.

Listening and vocabulary

Listening

1 ★★ 🔊 02 **Listen to a radio programme discussing how teenagers spend their time. Tick (✓) the things in the list they talk about.**

a	studying	✓
b	helping around the house	☐
c	social activities	☐
d	after-school activities	☐
e	holidays	☐
f	homework	☐
g	getting enough sleep	☐
h	clothes and fashion	☐

2 ★★ 🔊 02 **Listen again. Are these sentences true (*T*) or false (*F*)?**

1 The discussion topic is what teenagers
  do at school. *F*

2 Jamie doesn't do any extra activities. ___

3 He usually feels tired. ___

4 The teacher thinks her students do
  too much. ___

5 She says students should meet every
  evening to do homework. ___

6 The parent agrees with the teacher. ___

7 He thinks teenagers should concentrate
  on schoolwork. ___

8 The psychologist agrees with the teenager. ___

9 She thinks being with friends is important. ___

10 She says that helping around the house and
  sleeping are both important. ___

Performing

3 ★ **Complete the text with the words in the box.**

> dancing   orchestra   act   voice   play the piano
> ~~on stage~~   microphone   instruments

The concert last night was amazing. From the moment Jake came ¹___*on stage*___ everyone in the crowd was shouting, singing and ²_____ . There was a big ³_____ behind the band and the sound was incredible. Jake took the ⁴_____ and started singing 'Love is …'. He's got such a powerful ⁵_____ and all the girls screamed! During the concert he played different ⁶_____ and for the last song he sat down to ⁷_____ on his own. And there was a surprise at the end – he told everyone he's going to ⁸_____ in a film next month. He's a dream!

4 ★★★ **Use the words in Exercise 3 to make different words.**

1 We often make *microphone* shorter by seven letters.
  _____*mic*_____

2 Add *-al* to this word to describe a piece of music with
  no singing. _____

3 A person who dances. _____

4 A person who performs in a film or theatre.
  _____

5 Add *-l* to this word to describe music played by an
  orchestra. _____

6 A person who plays the piano. _____

7 Change this word to *voc-* and add *-al* and *-ist* for
  another word for a singer. _____

8 We also use this word as a verb to mean 'put on a
  performance'. _____

Language focus 2

(don't) have to

1 ⋆ **Complete the sentences in the box.**

> With *have to* we use ¹_____ or ²_____ to
> make negatives, and ³_____ or ⁴_____ to
> make questions.
> After *have/has to* we use the ⁵_____ form of
> the verb.
> Use *have/has to* to say that it is ⁶_____ to do
> something.
> Use *don't / doesn't have to* to say that it is
> not ⁷_____ to do something, but that you
> ⁸_____ do it if you want.

2 ⋆ (Circle) **the correct form of *have to* in
the sentences.**

Fashion ideas: *be yourself!*

1 It's essential to be yourself.
Remember people **have to /
(don't have to)** wear the same
clothes as everyone else!

2 You **have to / don't have to** look for
clothes or hairstyles which are a bit
different.

3 There are a lot of cheap shops, so teenagers
have to / don't have to spend a lot of money.

4 Everyone **has to / doesn't have to** experiment a
little to find their own style.

5 At school we **have to / don't have to** be careful
not to look too extreme!

6 You **have to / don't have to** follow fashion.
If you don't like it, don't wear it!

3 ⋆⋆ **Complete the conversation between the
PE teacher and a student with the correct
form of *have to* and the word in brackets.**

A: ¹ *Do I have to be* (I be) really fit to do a triathlon?

B: No, and ²_____ (you
be) very good at any of the individual sports.

A: ³_____ (beginners
swim) in open water, like a lake or the sea?

B: No, in all beginner races they swim in a pool.

A: ⁴_____ (I wear) a
helmet for the cycling part?

B: Yes, Every ⁵_____
(cyclist wear) a helmet to compete.

A: Do I need a racing bicycle?

B: No, ⁶_____ (your
bicycle be) a special one.

A: What about the running part?

B: ⁷_____ (every
competitor wear) a microchip on their shoe, for
their official time.

A: Right! Are the rules very complicated?

B: Yes, ⁸_____ (you read)
the rules carefully so you know what to do!

don't have to vs. mustn't

4 ⋆ **Complete the sentences with *don't have to*
or *mustn't*.**

1 We ___*don't have to*___ sing if you don't want to.

2 You _____ use your mobile phone while
you're driving.

3 Today's Friday so I _____ do my
homework.

4 You _____ forget to say good luck to
Dad. He's got a concert tonight.

5 She _____ use a microphone. I can hear
her perfectly.

6 She _____ be late for the concert or
they won't let her in.

(E)xplore prepositions

5 ⋆⋆ (Circle) **the correct words.**

1 There's a cinema (in front of) / **above** my uncle's
house. You can see it through the window.

2 Don't come in the house **over / until** I tell you to.

3 I try to balance my time **between / near** athletics
and homework.

4 We've got a big park **inside / behind** my house.

5 My school is **near / until** our house so I walk to
school every day.

6 The party was full **of / over** kids from his school.

7 You must be **until / over** 18 to watch this film.

8 Let's see who's taller. Stand **inside / beside** me
and we can see.

6 ⋆⋆⋆ **Imagine you are a rich and famous
person. How is your imaginary life different
from your real life? Write at least five
sentences about things you *have to* do now
and things you *don't have to* do.**

I'm a film star! I don't have to make my bed ...

Reading

1 ★ **Read about the problems a teenage athlete has. Complete the text with the headings in the box.**

> Diet   Schoolwork   ~~The attitude of my friends~~
> Getting enough sleep

BEING A TEENAGE ATHLETE

JUGGLING MY LIFE!   HOME   ABOUT   **BLOG**   CONTACT

I'm a long jumper. I train four times a week and compete on Sundays. I love athletics, but my life isn't easy and involves a lot of **juggling**. Schoolwork, training, family life, sleeping and socialising all need my attention and there are only 24 hours in a day! So what are my biggest problems?

1 *The attitude of my friends* : Most of my friends aren't **sporty** so they don't understand why I am. If we're hanging out and I have to leave early because I've got an **athletics meeting** on the next day, they say 'No, Sam, you mustn't go!'

2 _____ : An athlete can eat a lot and not get fat, but I must eat healthy food to support all the exercise (and **brainwork**!) I do. I have to ignore the machines selling sweets and chocolate (not easy!) and make sure I eat enormous **helpings** of protein, vegetables and fruit.

3 _____ : When I'm training hard I should go to bed early, or I quickly feel exhausted.

This is a problem, as I've sometimes got **loads of** homework to do when I get home. Luckily, there's Saturday!

4 _____ : I have to use every free moment. I often **revise** in the car to and from training. I do homework after dinner, but I shouldn't stay up late, so usually I finish my coursework at the weekend, when my friends are out having fun. I'm not surprised they think I'm crazy!

I don't have to do this, so why do I? Because I'm good at it, and I want to win a gold medal!

2 ★★ **Complete the sentences with the words in the box. Use the words in *bold* in the text to help you.**

> athletics meeting   revise   ~~loads of~~   helping (noun)
> brainwork   ignore   juggling   sporty

1 Another phrase for *lots of* is ____*loads of*____ .
2 If you _____ something, you act like it's not happening.
3 An _____ is an event where people compete in sports like running or jumping.
4 If you like playing sports you are a _____ person.
5 A _____ is a portion of food.
6 You have to think a lot when you do _____ .
7 To keep throwing three or four balls in the air, without dropping them is called _____ .
8 To _____ before an exam you read things you did in class and try to remember them.

3 ★★ **Choose the correct answers.**
1 How many times a week does Sam do athletics training?
   a five times a week
   ⓑ four times a week
2 Why can he eat a lot?
   a he does a lot of 'brainwork'
   b he doesn't get fat
3 What happens when he does a lot of training and he doesn't go to bed early?
   a he feels tired very quickly
   b he can't compete on Saturdays
4 How do Sam's friends feel about him?
   a they think he has fun
   b they think he's crazy

4 ★★★ **Write rules for Sam's life. Use *should/ shouldn't, must/mustn't* and *has to/doesn't have to* and the words in the box.**

> do homework   eat sweets and chocolate
> go to parties   eat a lot of protein
> stay up late   ~~train four times a week~~

1 *Sam has to train four times a week.*
2 _____
3 _____
4 _____
5 _____
6 _____

Writing

A competition entry

1 Read Mike's competition entry. Did he enjoy the camp?

WIN A VIDEO GAME

Write a review of an experience where you learned something new from using a computer. The best review will win a free video game!

Competition entry:

I love computer games, so I learned a lot from the two-week 'Game Design Summer Camp' I did this year. Everyone should try ¹ _it_ ! There were loads of ² _____ to choose from. My ³ _____ were the talks by professional game designers, and the gaming tournaments in the evenings and at weekends. And every afternoon we had outdoor activities, like swimming and volleyball. But the most important ⁴ _____ was designing a 3D video game. I did ⁵ _____ with my friends Carla and Sam – our instructors helped, of course! On the last day when we finished our games we had to present ⁶ _____ to a group of experts.

I was terrified, but ⁷ _____ were really nice. What did I learn? I learned how computer games work and I also learned how to do a good presentation. Not bad!

Mike

2 Read the competition entry again and match the questions with the answers.

1 What was the camp about?   _c_
2 When was it?   ___
3 How did Mike learn about computer games?   ___
4 What did they do in the evenings and at weekends? ___
5 What activities were there in the afternoon?   ___
6 Who did he design a game with?   ___
7 What did they do at the end of the course?   ___
8 What did Mike think of the course?   ___

a His friends Carla and Sam.
b There was information from professionals.
c How to design computer games.
d In the summer.
e They presented their game to experts.
f It was amazing.
g Sports and outdoor activities.
h Compete in computer games.

Useful language Avoiding repetition (1)

3 Complete Mike's competition entry with the words in the box.

> ~~it~~ this activities favourites one them they

4 Rewrite the sentences to avoid repetition. Use the text in Exercise 1 to help you.

1 I went to an amazing summer camp. The camp was about performing and acting.
   I went to an amazing summer camp. It was about performing and acting.

2 There were lots of activities but my favourite activities were juggling and singing.
   _____

3 I sang a song and then my friend sang a song by One Direction.
   _____

4 We tried juggling but juggling is really difficult.
   _____

5 There were big helpings of vegetables but I didn't eat the helpings of vegetables.
   _____

6 All the students on the camp were the same age as me and all the students were really good actors.
   _____

Writing

5 Complete the sentences with the correct prepositions.

1 There were loads ____*of*____ activities to try.
2 We had a chance to hang out _____ people from different countries.
3 Sailing camp was perfect _____ me.
4 You choose _____ six activities.
5 At night we sat _____ a fire singing.
6 We went into town to shop _____ souvenirs.

> **WRITING TIP**
> Make it better! ✓ ✓ ✓
> Use time expressions but be careful with articles and prepositions.

6 Choose the correct time expressions.

1 We played basketball in / (in the) afternoons.
2 There were different activities at / in the night.
3 Most people went home in / at weekends.
4 The activities finished at / to 4 o'clock.
5 On / In the first day, we got into groups.
6 They put on films at every night / every night.

> **WRITING TIP**
> Make it better! ✓ ✓ ✓
> Use transition words to join sentences and ideas.

7 Complete the competition entry with the words in the box.

> of course   And then   Actually
> ~~In fact~~   So far   For instance

Before I went to surf camp last summer, I didn't like the sea. ¹____*In fact*____ , I hated it! However, the camp was amazing and, ²_____ I had a great time. There were lots of activities. ³_____ , you could try windsurfing or kitesurfing. ⁴_____ if you didn't want to go in the water, you could learn about surfboards. ⁵_____ surfboards are difficult to take care of. ⁶_____ it's the best camp I've been on.

8 Read the competition entry again. Tick (✓) the things in the list that Mike writes about.

the daytime/night/weekend activities ☐
the instructors / other campers ☐
the daily routine ☐
why you liked it ☐
the food ☐
the weather ☐

PLAN

9 Read about the competition in the box. Use the headings in Exercise 8 or your own ideas to make notes.

ACTIVITY CAMP COMPETITION

Win a *FREE* activity camp for two weeks!

Write about an activity camp that you went to. What sort of camp was it? The best description will win two weeks at the best activity camp in the world!

WRITE

10 Write your competition entry. Look at page 27 of the Student's Book to help you.

_____
_____
_____
_____
_____
_____
_____
_____
_____
_____
_____
_____
_____
_____
_____
_____

CHECK

11 Check your writing. Can you say YES to these questions?

• Is there any repetition in your competition entry?
• Do you use transition words between ideas and sentences?
• Are the prepositions correct?
• Do you use time expressions correctly?
• Are the spelling and punctuation correct?

Do you need to write a second draft?

Vocabulary
Priorities

1 Match the phrases with the examples.

1	chatting with friends online	a	going to bed early
2	hanging out with friends	b	using Facebook or Twitter to send messages to friends
3	shopping for clothes	c	going to a café to be with your friends
4	helping around the house	d	buying new shoes and jeans
5	getting enough sleep	e	playing for your school basketball team
6	having time for yourself	f	reading a book in your room
7	doing something creative	g	designing computer games
8	doing sports	h	cleaning your room and doing the washing-up

Total: 7

Performing

2 Put the letters in brackets in order to make words.

1 I can't hear you. Could you speak into the _microphone_ ? (poochminer)
2 To work on the radio, you have to have a nice _____ . (icove).
3 He always gets very nervous before he goes on _____ . (gsate).
4 Listening to an _____ live is amazing. (aeothsrcr)
5 We're going _____ on Friday. (gnadinc)
6 OK, you can sing and dance. But can you _____? (tca)
7 She played all the _____ on her last album. (ssmettnnur)
8 My grandmother plays the _____ and she's 85. (oniap)

Total: 7

Language focus
should/must

3 Complete the letters with should or shouldn't.

Dear Abby,
I have problems getting enough sleep. My parents say I ¹ _should_ go to bed earlier. My best friend told me I ² _____ eat so much chocolate. My sister says I ³ _____ listen to relaxing music before I go to bed. What do you think? What ⁴ _____ I do?
'Worried'

Dear 'Worried',
There are many reasons for not getting enough sleep. You ⁵ _____ worry about it, because worrying can keep you awake. You also ⁶ _____ eat dinner late, and you ⁷ _____ try drinking some herbal tea before you go to bed.
Abby

Total: 6

4 Match the sentences and complete them with must or mustn't.

1	You look so tired.	a	You _____ eat some lunch.
2	You look hungry.	b	You _____ hurry!
3	You're really late!	c	I _____ forget to buy her a card.
4	It's Mum's birthday tomorrow.	d	We _____ be late.
5	The concert is at 6 pm.	e	You _mustn't_ go to bed late.
6	I need to finish my Science project.	f	I _____ do it this weekend.

Total: 5

(don't) have to vs. mustn't

5 Complete the sentences. Use don't have to, doesn't have to or mustn't.

1 At my school you _don't have to_ wear a uniform.
2 Be careful, you _____ drop the glasses!
3 My brother is only four years old, so he _____ help around the house.
4 On Sundays we _____ get up early.
5 Tomorrow I have PE at school, so I _____ forget to bring my sports clothes.

Total: 4

Language builder

6 (Circle) the correct options.

> **Gina:** What **¹**___ last weekend?
> **Alex:** I **²**___ my dog for a long walk. How about you?
> **Gina:** I **³**___ a marathon. But when we **⁴**___ , it **⁵**___ to rain and we all got wet!
> **Alex:** Oh, dear! **⁶**___ every day?
> **Gina:** Before running a marathon, I **⁷**___ every morning.
> **Alex:** Wow! You **⁸**___ tired sometimes. **⁹**___ eat a special diet?
> **Gina:** Not really, I just eat lots of vegetables and fruit and I **¹⁰**___ eat sweets or chocolates. Do you want to go running with me?
> **Alex:** OK. But first I **¹¹**___ to find my running shoes!

1	**(a)** did you do	**b** you did do	**c** you did
2	**a** was taking	**b** took	**c** take
3	**a** running	**b** was running	**c** ran
4	**a** were running	**b** ran	**c** run
5	**a** start	**b** was starting	**c** started
6	**a** Do you run	**b** You do run	**c** You run
7	**a** run usually	**b** usually running	**c** usually run
8	**a** must feel	**b** should feel	**c** did
9	**a** You have to	**b** You do have to	**c** Do you have to
10	**a** mustn't	**b** don't have to	**c** 'm not eating
11	**a** must	**b** should	**c** have

Total: 10

Vocabulary builder

7 (Circle) the correct options.
1 It was cold, so the rain turned into ___ .
   (a) hail   **b** thunder   **c** heat wave
2 Sing into the ___ . I can't hear you.
   a piano   **b** microphone   **c** orchestra
3 It was -3 °C – the temperature was below ___ .
   a freezing   **b** boiling   **c** lightning
4 I study all the time. ___ is so important.
   a Fashion   **b** Education   **c** Transport
5 When you cross the road you need to look ___ both directions.
   a of   **b** on   **c** in
6 We need to take a ___ because it will be dark at night.
   a compass   **b** torch   **c** camera
7 Pack a ___ because it can be cold at night.
   a sleeping bag   **b** water bottle   **c** map
8 I like sports ___ , like football and tennis matches.
   a games   **b** networks   **c** events
9 I don't usually stay ___ late at the weekend.
   a on   **b** out   **c** after
10 That new film is really scary – I was ___ .
   a terrified   **b** stressed   **c** exhausted

Total: 9

Speaking

8 Put the words in the correct order to make phrases for helping someone to do something.
1 show / Let / you / me
   Let me show you.
2 know / you / to / it / how / Do / do ?
   _____
3 good / very / at / not / I'm / Maths
   _____
4 hand / give / you / I'll / a / like / you / if
   _____
5 kind / really / That / 's
   _____
6 very / It / really / simple / 's
   _____

Total: 5

Total: 53

should/must

> Remember that:
> • we use the infinitive without *to* after *should/ shouldn't* and *must/mustn't*
>   ✓ You shouldn't go to bed late the night before an exam.
>   ✗ You shouldn't ~~to~~ go to bed late the night before an exam.

1 Find and correct five more mistakes with *should* and *must* in the rules.

IF THERE IS A FIRE IN YOUR HOME ...

1. You mustn't ~~to~~ panic! You should concentrate and breathe slowly.
2. You should to make sure everybody in the house is awake.
3. You must leave the house as quickly as possible.
4. If you can see smoke under the door, you mustn't to open it.
5. If the door is hot, you must to find another way to leave.
6. You should find a door that goes to the outside.
7. When you are out of the house, you must to telephone for help.
8. You shouldn't to go back into the house for any reason.

have to

> Remember that:
> • we don't usually use the contracted form of *have* with *have to*
>   ✓ On Saturdays, I have to help with the shopping.
>   ✗ On Saturdays, I've to help with the shopping.
> • we use the infinitive without *to* after *(don't) have to*
>   ✓ I have to look after my younger brother.
>   ✗ I have to ~~looking~~ after my younger brother.
>   ✗ I have to ~~looked~~ after my younger brother.
> • we use *have* after *I/you/we/they,* and *has* after *he/ she/it*
>   ✓ My grandmother has to go to the hospital.
>   ✗ My grandmother ~~have~~ to go to the hospital.

2 Find and correct six more mistakes with *have to* in the email.

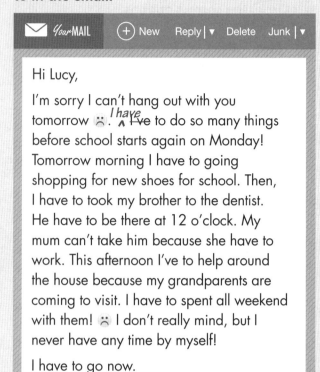

Hi Lucy,

I'm sorry I can't hang out with you tomorrow ☹. ˄*I have* I've to do so many things before school starts again on Monday! Tomorrow morning I have to going shopping for new shoes for school. Then, I have to took my brother to the dentist. He have to be there at 12 o'clock. My mum can't take him because she have to work. This afternoon I've to help around the house because my grandparents are coming to visit. I have to spent all weekend with them! ☹ I don't really mind, but I never have any time by myself!

I have to go now.

Bye!

Claire

need to

> • we use the infinitive with *to* after *need*
>   ✓ I need to be alone sometimes.
>   ✗ I ~~need be~~ alone sometimes.
>   ✗ I ~~need being~~ alone sometimes.

3 Circle the correct option.
1. There are three things you need **remember /** (**to remember**) for the exam.
2. To get to sleep, you need **to feel / feeling** relaxed.
3. You really need **catch / to catch** up on your sleep. You're studying too hard.
4. You need **doing / to do** more exercise.
5. Teenagers need **to get / get** at least eight hours of sleep every night.
6. I need **to help / helping** my dad tomorrow.

3 Art all around us

Vocabulary

Art around us

1 ★ **Put the letters in order to make words connected with the arts.**

rotcenc lalh   kurbse   rejglug   vlinig usteat
troipart intreap   raygell   laurm   fatigrif
ebnithoxii   rutspluce

1	_concert hall_	6	_____
2	_____	7	_____
3	_____	8	_____
4	_____	9	_____
5	_____	10	_____

2 ★ **Write the vocabulary from Exercise 1 in the correct place.**

1 Two buildings used for the arts:
  concert hall, _____

2 Three people you see in the street:
  _____

3 Two things you can see on an outside wall:
  _____

4 Two things you see in a gallery:
  _____

5 A person who paints people: _____

3 ★★ **Complete the sentences. Use vocabulary from Exercise 1.**

1 My school had a lot of ugly _graffiti_ on the outside wall, so they asked the students to paint a(n) _____ instead.

2 The Picasso _____ in Berlin this summer is very popular. It's difficult to get tickets.

3 There are often _____ in the New York subway. People like hearing music in the stations.

4 The Ramblas in Barcelona is famous for its _____ _____ . They don't move for hours.

5 We've got a(n) _____ _____ in my town but it's all classical music, so I don't go.

6 The Louvre is a museum and art _____ in Paris.

4 ★★ **Read the clues and write the words.**

1 These can be music students who need money.   _buskers_

2 These can be metal, stone or plastic.   _____

3 They need to practise so things don't fall.   _____

4 You usually have to pay for music here. _____

5 This person often copies a photo of someone.   _____

6 This often lasts for several months.   _____

5 ★★★ **Write answers to the questions.**

1 Which of the things on this page _haven't_ you got where you live?

2 What do you think of graffiti?

3 What kind of street performers do you watch?

4 Have you got any paintings at home? What are they of?

Language focus 1

Present perfect for indefinite past time

1 ★ (Circle) the correct options.

1 Famous musicians like Bob Dylan, Paul McCartney and Bon Jovi (have performed) / has performed as buskers (but they didn't make a lot of money!).

2 That juggler **is dropped / has dropped** a ball every time I **'ve watched / 'm watched** him perform. He isn't very good!

3 Alan **never has enjoyed / has never enjoyed** going to exhibitions of classical paintings.

4 Sometimes living statues suddenly move. It surprises you if you **haven't to notice / haven't noticed** them before.

5 A local youth group **has painted / is paint** several murals on the outside of the cultural centre.

2 ★★ Complete the sentences with the correct form of the verbs in the box. Use the present perfect affirmative or negative.

> meet take win see be ~~speak~~

1 We ____have spoken____ to the teachers about painting a mural in the dining room at school.

2 My parents _____ me to any galleries so I _____ a lot of art.

3 One Dutch man _____ the living statues World Championships three times.

4 She works in a record company so she _____ a lot of musicians.

5 My favourite bands _____ to my town because we haven't got a concert hall.

3 ★★ Complete the text with the present perfect form of the verbs in brackets.

Banksy, the world famous graffiti artist, is a mystery man. He ¹ _has never revealed_ (never reveal) his real name and ² _____ (create) murals all over the world. Banksy paints quickly so the police ³ _____ (never catch) him. He's a street artist, but people ⁴ _____ (buy) his work for thousands of pounds. He ⁵ _____ (paint) portraits too, like Kate Moss and Queen Victoria (now owned by Christina Aguilera). Banksy ⁶ _____ (make) a lot of money from his art, and his work ⁷ _____ (increase) interest in street art in general.

4 ★★★ Write at least five sentences about your experiences with art and music. Use the words in the box or your own ideas, and verbs in the present perfect.

> see an art exhibition   paint a mural
> go to a concert hall   see living statues
> paint graffiti   give money to a busker

(E)xplore collocations

5 ★★ Complete the sentences with the words in the box.

> make posted ~~taking~~ about at hard

1 Maddy has always liked _____taking_____ photos.

2 I've never been very good _____ painting.

3 We made a funny video and I've _____ it online.

4 My mum and dad work very _____ . They're both doctors.

5 Our teacher is really passionate _____ opera. She always plays music in class.

6 I don't think the most important thing in life is to _____ money.

Listening and vocabulary

Instruments

1 ★ **Write the words.**

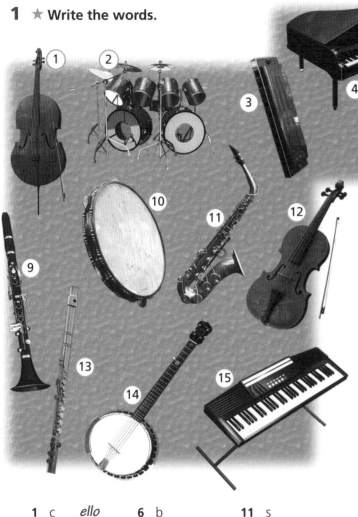

1 c__*ello*__   6 b_____   11 s_____
2 d_____   7 r_____   12 v_____
3 m_____   8 t_____   13 f_____
   o_____   9 c_____   14 b_____
4 p_____   10 t_____   15 k_____
5 g_____

2 ★★ **Answer the questions with words from Exercise 1. Not all the words are needed.**

1 Which instruments can you find in a rock band?
   *keyboards,*_____

2 Which instruments do children often play in primary school?
   _____

3 Which instruments are often played in jazz?
   _____

4 Which instruments can you see in an orchestra?
   _____

5 Which instruments are difficult to play in the street?
   _____

Listening

3 ★ 🔊 **03** **Listen to a radio interview with two street performers. What do they do?**

> living statue juggler jazz musician
> magician fire-eater bongo-drummer

Greg is a _____ and Alice is a _____ .

4 ★ 🔊 **03** **Listen again. Circle the correct options.**

1 Greg decided to do his job when he was **fifteen** / **sixteen** .

2 He first thought of doing it at a **music festival** / **street carnival** .

3 He **was** / **wasn't** a good magician when he first started.

4 He's performed **only in Europe** / **in many different countries** .

5 He likes **the lifestyle** / **lots of people watching him** .

6 Alice thinks juggling with fire **is** / **isn't** dangerous.

7 She has worked in a **circus school** / **circus** .

8 She **always** / **sometimes** works at night.

9 She can make a lot of money **in a short time** / **at night** .

10 There are **a lot of** / **a few** women street performers in Covent Garden.

Language focus 2

Present perfect with *ever/never*

1 ★ Circle the correct options.
1 I have **ever** / **never** given money to a busker.
2 Have you **ever** / **never** tried to juggle?
3 My dad **has played never** / **has never played** the piano.
4 Tanya **has never seen** / **never has seen** a living statue.
5 **Has your teacher ever** / **Has ever your teacher** taken you to a gallery?
6 I **never have** / **have never** been to that concert hall.

2 ★★ Put the words in order to make questions and sentences.
1 your family/ made / you / for / Have / ever / dinner / ?
Have you ever made dinner for your family?

2 visited / ever / the Tate Gallery / they / Have / ?
_____

3 ever / she / Has / a live concert / seen / ?
_____

4 never / a famous person. / met / She's
_____

5 never / that book. / read / I've
_____

6 helped / me. / never / You've
_____

3 ★ Write present perfect questions and the correct answers. ✓ = yes and ✗ = no.
1 your friend / ever / listen to / an opera? ✓
Has your friend ever listened to an opera?
Yes, she has.

2 your parents / ever / go to / a music festival? ✗
_____
_____

3 she / hear / of the escape artist Houdini? ✗
_____
_____

4 the students / finish / their art project? ✓
_____
_____

5 you and your friends / ever / see / a famous band? ✓
_____
_____

6 you / listen to / their new CD? ✗
_____
_____

4 ★★★ Write answers to the questions. Use the present perfect.
1 What exhibitions have you been to?
_____
_____

2 Has anyone you know ever performed in public?
_____
_____

3 What TV series have you followed?
_____
_____

4 What famous bands have you seen?
_____
_____

5 What creative things have you done?
_____
_____

I've been to a modern art exhibition, a street art exhibition, ...

Explore phrasal verbs with *up*

5 ★★ Match the sentence halves.
1 My mum says I can't go out   *d*
2 They pressed the button   ___
3 We missed the start of the film   ___
4 The photographer set up his camera   ___
5 We had a party   ___
6 We can't have dinner   ___

a and started taking photos.
b because Jacob showed up late.
c and we all dressed up as superheroes.
d until I tidy up my room.
e because Adam hasn't picked up the food.
f and thousands of small lights lit up the streets.

Reading

1 ★ **Read the text about being a living statue. Is it a difficult job?**

Being a
LIVING STATUE

Nowadays you see living statues all over the world. They wear elaborate **costumes** and body paint, and stand without moving for hours. But what's it like? Is it difficult? I spoke to Nina, a living statue in London.

'You need to be physically and mentally **fit**. It's actually quite hard standing **still**, and you have to eat before you start or you feel ill.

'We wear body paint so we look like real metal or **stone** statues. Metallic paint takes over an hour to put on and it's difficult to **get off**, too. Every week I have a sauna to clean my skin. I love designing different costumes and being creative. We even paint our clothes to make them look heavy. In the winter you need to wear thermal underwear under your costume so you don't **shiver** with cold.

'I've worked at glamorous birthday parties for famous people, and in parks in the rain, and I've just been to the World Championships in Holland. There were 300 statues and 300,000 visitors. It was incredible! Most people love us but sometimes young children are frightened and I've seen one or two cry!'

Antonio Santos from Barcelona holds the world record for standing still, an incredible 20 hours, 11 minutes and 38 seconds, but the longest Nina has stood without moving is two and a half hours, at a party. 'It was awful! So now, I move. If someone gives me money, I **blow a kiss** or do a dance to say thank you. And of course if you need to **sneeze** or something, you have to 'come alive' and make it part of the performance. It's hard work but fun!'

2 ★★ **Complete the sentences with the words in the box. Use the words in *bold* in the text to help you.**

> blow a kiss   sneeze   costume   ~~stone~~   get off
> shiver   fit [*adjective*]   still [*adjective*]

1 That ___stone___ flowerpot looks great but it's really heavy.
2 Did he wear a pirate _____ for Carnival?
3 Oh! I want to _____ but I can't. It's a horrible feeling.
4 I always _____ to my granny when we leave her house to drive home.
5 I think this paint on my T-shirt is permanent. It's impossible to _____ .
6 My cousin is very active. She can't sit _____ for one minute.
7 It was freezing outside and we started to _____ .
8 My mum goes running to stay _____ .

3 ★★ **Read the text again. Are these sentences true (*T*) or false (*F*)? Correct the false sentences.**

1 You can only see living statues in Europe. *F*
   They are all over the world.
2 Living statues need to use their mind and their body.
   _____
3 The paint is easy to put on and get off.
   _____
4 Nina works in lots of different places.
   _____
5 Lots of people are scared of the living statues.
   _____
6 Nina doesn't enjoy her job.
   _____

4 ★★★ **Read the sentences. Tick (✓) the ones a living statue probably says. What does the other person do?**

1 'I'm wearing three T-shirts under my costume – it's really cold.' ✓
2 'I sometimes drop a ball when I try with six.' ☐
3 'A little girl started crying when she saw me.' ☐
4 'A bird landed on my head today.' ☐
5 'Sometimes I stand on one leg and do it with three knives.' ☐
6 'I'm going for a sauna now to wash the paint off.' ☐

5 ★★★ **Imagine working as a living statue. What is good about it? What are the difficult things? Write your ideas.**

Writing

An Internet post

1 Read Pete's Internet post. How many different types of performers does he write about?

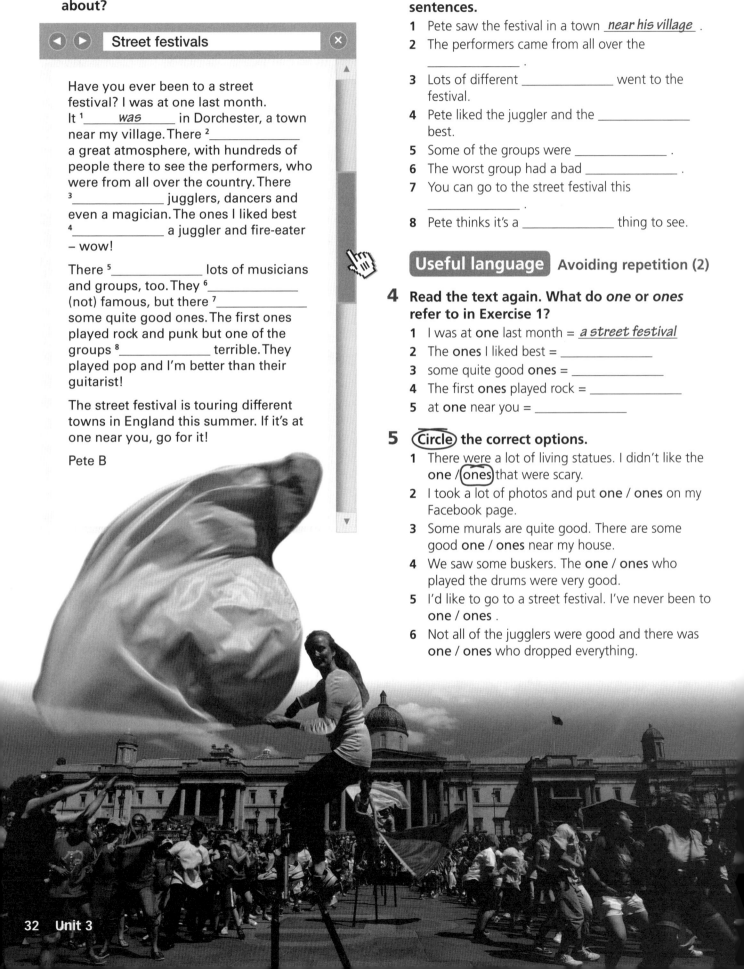

◀ ▶ **Street festivals** ✕

Have you ever been to a street festival? I was at one last month. It ¹____was____ in Dorchester, a town near my village. There ²_____ a great atmosphere, with hundreds of people there to see the performers, who were from all over the country. There ³_____ jugglers, dancers and even a magician. The ones I liked best ⁴_____ a juggler and fire-eater – wow!

There ⁵_____ lots of musicians and groups, too. They ⁶_____ (not) famous, but there ⁷_____ some quite good ones. The first ones played rock and punk but one of the groups ⁸_____ terrible. They played pop and I'm better than their guitarist!

The street festival is touring different towns in England this summer. If it's at one near you, go for it!

Pete B

---

2 Complete the Internet post with the correct forms of the verb *be*.

3 Read the Internet post again. Complete the sentences.

1 Pete saw the festival in a town _near his village_ .
2 The performers came from all over the _____ .
3 Lots of different _____ went to the festival.
4 Pete liked the juggler and the _____ best.
5 Some of the groups were _____ .
6 The worst group had a bad _____ .
7 You can go to the street festival this _____ .
8 Pete thinks it's a _____ thing to see.

> **Useful language** Avoiding repetition (2)

4 Read the text again. What do *one* or *ones* refer to in Exercise 1?

1 I was at **one** last month = _a street festival_
2 The **ones** I liked best = _____
3 some quite good **ones** = _____
4 The first **ones** played rock = _____
5 at **one** near you = _____

5 ⊙ Circle the correct options.

1 There were a lot of living statues. I didn't like the **one** / **ones** that were scary.
2 I took a lot of photos and put **one** / **ones** on my Facebook page.
3 Some murals are quite good. There are some good **one** / **ones** near my house.
4 We saw some buskers. The **one** / **ones** who played the drums were very good.
5 I'd like to go to a street festival. I've never been to **one** / **ones** .
6 Not all of the jugglers were good and there was **one** / **ones** who dropped everything.

Writing

6 Rewrite the sentences. Put the words in brackets in the correct place.

1 There were buskers and there were some amazing jugglers. (too)
There were buskers and there were some amazing jugglers, too.

2 There was a busker who played 10 different instruments! (even)

_____
_____

3 We went to an exhibition and we saw some portrait painters. (also)

_____
_____

4 I've seen a busker who played the mouth organ. (never)

_____
_____

5 Have you seen a street magician? (ever)

_____
_____

7 (Circle) the correct options.

1 He was **the more amazing /(the most amazing)** juggler I've ever seen.

2 I'm a **better / best** keyboard player than him!

3 I've never seen a **worse / worst** living statue!

4 The busker I liked **better / best** was a young girl who played the saxophone.

5 He dressed up as a sheep – it was the **funnier / funniest** costume I've ever seen.

6 I've never seen a **better / best** portrait.

> **WRITING TIP**
>
> Make it better! ✓ ✓ ✓
> Make a recommendation at the end of your Internet post to the reader.

8 Read the sentences. Which one is <u>not</u> a recommendation?

1 If it comes to your town, go for it!

2 The exhibition is amazing. You shouldn't miss it!

3 I think everybody should go and see this festival.

4 There were lots of great things to do.

5 When it comes to your town, you can't miss it!

9 Put the information in the order it appears in the Internet post in Exercise 1.

> the audience   the performers
> writer's opinion of artists   ~~where it was~~
> favourite performer   recommendation

1 *where it was* _____
2 _____
3 _____
4 _____
5 _____
6 _____

PLAN

10 Invent a street festival. Make notes for each heading in Exercise 9.

WRITE

11 Write an Internet post about your festival. Look at page 39 of the Student's Book to help you.

_____
_____
_____
_____
_____
_____
_____
_____
_____
_____
_____
_____
_____
_____

CHECK

12 Check your writing. Can you say YES to these questions?

• Is the information from Exercise 9 in your description?

• Do you use *one* or *ones* to avoid repetition?

• Do you use comparatives and superlatives correctly?

• Are words like *too, even, ever, also* and *never* in the correct place in the sentences?

• Do you make a recommendation at the end?

• Are the spelling and punctuation correct?

Do you need to write a second draft?

Vocabulary
Art around us

1 (Circle) the correct options.

1 A busker plays music ___ .
   (a) on the street   **b** in a concert hall
2 A portrait painter paints pictures of ___ .
   a people   **b** places
3 You usually see graffiti in ___ .
   a the street   **b** a museum
4 A juggler ___ .
   a makes paintings and sculptures
   b throws and catches objects
5 You can listen to music in ___ .
   a a concert hall   **b** a gallery
6 You go to a gallery to see ___ .
   a an exhibition   **b** a concert
7 The ___ moved because I gave it money.
   a juggler   **b** living statue
8 The grey wall was boring, so we painted ___ .
   a a mural   **b** an exhibition

Total: 7

Instruments

2 Put the letters in order to make musical instruments.

1 ratuig   _guitar_
2 drcerore   _____
3 lnterica   _____
4 poxeshano   _____
5 niolvi   _____
6 murtept   _____
7 bronautemi   _____
8 leutf   _____
9 ngobso   _____
10 roasbdyke   _____

Total: 9

Language focus
Present perfect for indefinite past time

3 Match the sentence halves.

1 She's never performed
2 My brother has worked as
3 I'm sorry but I haven't finished
4 I haven't noticed
5 They've painted a
6 We've watched

a my homework.
b mural outside the library.
c in public before.
d any graffiti where I live.
e all the Harry Potter films.
f a busker in New York.

Total: 5

4 Complete the text with the present perfect form of the verbs in brackets.

I ¹ _'ve_ always ____wanted____ (want) to have a band and now I do. I ² _____ (ask) some friends to join, too. Mark ³ _____ (play) the guitar with two other bands. Julie ⁴ _____ (never sing) with a band, but she's got a fantastic voice. We ⁵ _____ (not give) any concerts, but we ⁶ _____ (practise) a lot. We ⁷ _____ (begin) to write some songs and we ⁸ _____ (send) a demo recording to some music companies!

Total: 7

Present perfect with *ever/never*

5 Write present perfect sentences and questions with *ever* and *never*.

1 I / see / a famous band ✗
   I've never seen a famous band.
2 you / be / to a concert?
   _____
3 your brother / meet / a famous person?
   _____
4 they / be / to Russia ✗
   _____
5 she / eat / meat?
   _____
6 we / see / the sea ✗
   _____

Total: 5

Language builder

6 Complete the conversation with the missing words. Circle the correct options.

> **Isabel:** ¹___ played any musical instruments?
> **John:** Yes, I ²___ to play the banjo.
> **Isabel:** That's interesting. I ³___ the banjo.
> **John:** I ⁴___ to a music festival last year. Some buskers ⁵___ the banjo and I liked the sound.
> **Isabel:** Is it difficult?
> **John:** Not really, but you ⁶___ to practise every day.
> **Isabel:** I want to learn a musical instrument, too. What ⁷___ play?
> **John:** Well, first you ⁸___ decide what kind of music you want to play.
> **Isabel:** I want to play rock music. I ⁹___ of buying drums but they're very expensive. And ¹⁰___ find a teacher?
> **John:** You ¹¹___ do that now – you can practise by yourself first.

1	ⓐ Have you ever	**b** Did you	**c** Were you
2	**a** learn	**b** 'm learning	**c** did learn
3	**a** 've never tried	**b** never have tried	**c** 've tried never
4	**a** go	**b** was going	**c** went
5	**a** have played	**b** were playing	**c** are playing
6	**a** mustn't	**b** should	**c** have
7	**a** I should	**b** should I	**c** do I should
8	**a** should	**b** shouldn't	**c** have
9	**a** think	**b** thought	**c** was thinking
10	**a** have I to	**b** I do have to	**c** do I have to
11	**a** don't have to	**b** not have to	**c** mustn't

Total: 10

Vocabulary builder

7 Circle the correct options.

1 It's freezing outside. You'll ___ a cold.
  a take   ⓑ catch   **c** make
2 It's very dark. Have you got a ___ ?
  a torch   **b** map   **c** penknife
3 There was a huge ___ on the wall with lots of colours.
  a busker   **b** exhibition   **c** mural
4 Abby was afraid of the ___ and lightning.
  a hail   **b** snowstorm   **c** thunder
5 Before you go out in the sun put on some ___ .
  a sun cream   **b** glasses   **c** conditions
6 You should help ___ the house and tidy your room.
  a for   **b** around   **c** through
7 We'll wait ___ Lily comes.
  a near   **b** over   **c** until
8 A ___ is like a big violin.
  a cello   **b** clarinet   **c** piano
9 There were about 200 people ___ total.
  a on   **b** to   **c** in
10 I waited at the cinema for an hour and he never ___ up.
  a picked   **b** set   **c** showed

Total: 9

Speaking

8 Put the sentences in the correct order to make a conversation.

___ **Sally:** How about meeting at my house at 6.30?
___ **Lynn:** OK. See you later.
___ **Sally:** Yeah, why not?
_1_ **Lynn:** Do you fancy going out for pizza later?
___ **Lynn:** I can't meet until 7, sorry.
___ **Sally:** Sounds good! Shall I ask my dad to pick you up?
___ **Lynn:** What time shall we meet then?

Total: 6

Total: 58

Get it right! Unit 3

Present perfect with *been/gone*

1 **Find and correct three more mistakes with *been* and *gone*.**

I wanted to have a party on Saturday, but no one can come! Mary has ~~been~~ *gone* to London with her family, so she can't come. Paul has gone to France for two weeks and isn't coming back until next Friday. Clara has gone skiing, so she can't come. And I don't know about Tia. I've gone to her house, but there was no one home. Maybe she's gone to visit her grandparents. I phoned Leonardo and he hasn't been anywhere, but he's ill in bed at home! Even my brother has been on holiday until next week. I think I'm going to have to have my party another day!

Present perfect with *ever/never*

Remember that:
- we use *ever* in present perfect questions when the exact time isn't important
  - ✓ *Have you ever played at this festival?*
- we don't usually use *never* in questions
  - ✓ *Have you ever played at this festival?*
  - ✗ *Have you never played at this festival?*
- we use *never* to say 'not at any time'. It isn't used with *not/n't*.
  - ✓ *He has never visited England.*
  - ✗ *He hasn't never visited England.*
- we put *never* and *ever* between *have* and the past participle
  - ✓ *I have never played in a group.*
  - ✗ *I never have played in a group.*
  - ✗ *Have ever you played in a group?*

2 **Are the sentences correct? Correct the incorrect sentences.**
1 I haven't never been to a festival.
   I have never been to a festival.
2 Have ever you sung in a choir or group?
3 She has never seen a living statue.
4 Has he never played in an orchestra?

5 They never have visited an art gallery.

6 He hasn't never met a famous person.

Collocations

Remember that:
- different verbs go with different nouns. Don't use the wrong verb!
  - ✓ *Have you done your homework?*
  - ✗ *Have you made your homework?*
  - ✓ *I made a lot of mistakes in the exam.*
  - ✗ *I did a lot of mistakes in the exam.*

3 **Put the words and phrases in the correct place in the table.**

~~a drawing~~   a presentation   photos   art   money   a work of art   graffiti   copies of something

Do	Make	Take
a drawing		

Spell it right! Past participles

Remember that:
- we form the present perfect with subject + have(n't)/has(n't) + past participle. We don't use the past simple.
- with irregular verbs, the past simple form of the verb and the past participle are often different. Look at the irregular verb table on page 126 of the Student's Book.
  - ✓ *I have never taken a really cool photo.*
  - ✓ *I have never ~~took~~ a really cool photo.*

4 **Write the correct past simple and past participle form of the verbs.**

Infinitive	Past simple	Past participle
take	*took*	*taken*
give		
speak		
do		
know		
sing		

4 Adventure

Vocabulary

Expressions with *go*

1 ★ **Use the clues to complete the crossword.**

```
          1
          |
          |
          |
          |      2       3
4 s a i l i n g
          |
          5
          |
          |          6
          |
          7
```

Across

4 You need a boat and a good wind for this activity.
5 You can go on rides if you go here.
6 You can do this inside on a wall, or outside in the mountains.
7 You do this in snow in the mountains in winter.

Down

1 You do this kind of visit with another school.
2 Young people often stay in this place in the summer holidays.
3 You do this type of long walk in the mountains.
4 Going on one of these is a good way to see wild animals.
5 You do this with a guide who shows you a place and tells you about it.

2 ★ **Match the verbs with the nouns in Exercise 1.**

1 Things you go on: a ___safari___ , a school _____ , a guided _____
2 Activities with go: _____ , _____ , _____ ,
3 A thing you go to: summer _____ , _____

3 ★★ **Complete the email about Gemma's summer. Use the complete nouns from Exercise 2.**

| ✉ *Your* MAIL | ⊕ New Reply ▼ Delete |

Hi Uncle Rob,
I have a problem this summer and I don't know what to do. All my friends are doing something exciting. Joe is going to a 1 ___theme park___ in California for a week. Maria is going to 2 _____ in Wales to do rafting with her sister. She loves camping, and she's bought new mountain boots for when they go 3 _____ . It sounds fun! Alex is unhappy because his parents have decided to go to Greece. His mum wants to go on a 4 _____ of ancient ruins – boring! Emma has gone to Tanzania on a 5 _____ with her grandparents. Isn't that amazing? I wanted to visit my friend in Germany (do you remember she came here on a 6 _____ in May?), but she's gone rock 7 _____ in the Alps – too dangerous for me! Anyway, Mum and Dad want to go 8 _____ in Colorado (there's snow there in August!), but I want to go to the beach. Can I come and stay in Menorca with you and my cousins like last year? We could go 9 _____ in your little boat again. It would be fantastic.
What do you think?
Love,
Gemma

1 ATTATCHMENT
💾 Save
🗑 Delete

4 ★★★ **What are your favourite holiday activities? Have you ever done any of the things in Exercise 1? Write at least five sentences. Use a dictionary if necessary.**

I've never been on a cruise but I think it would be fun.

Language focus 1

Present perfect with *still*, *yet*, *already* and *just*

1 ★ **Complete the sentences with the present perfect and *just*. Use the verbs in brackets.**

1 'What's that CD?'
'I _'ve just bought___ it from a great busker in town.' (buy)

2 'What are those kids doing?' 'Juggling! They _____ how to do it!' (learn)

3 'Be careful! We _____ this door.' (paint)

4 'He looks tired.' 'Yes, he _____ a marathon!' (finish)

5 'What are you watching?' 'A film. I _____ it.' (download)

6 'Where did you put my book? I know you _____ it!' (move)

2 ★ **Circle the correct options.**

1 We haven't gone to the theme park **still** / **yet**. It's next week.

2 Nicky **still** / **already** hasn't packed for her school exchange visit tomorrow!

3 Have you put on suncream **yet** / **still** today?

4 We arrived on Saturday and I've **already** / **still** been sailing twice. It's great!

5 They've **already** / **yet** decided which mountain to climb, I think.

6 My grandparents **yet** / **still** haven't arrived home after their guided tour of Colombia.

3 ★★ **Put the words in the correct order to make sentences.**

1 your / been / yet / you / Have / exchange / on / school?
Have you been on your school exchange yet?

2 Brigitte / arrived / already / has / my / at / house
_____

3 climbing / started / I / haven't / the / still / course
_____

4 yet / castle / haven't / the / seen / They
_____

5 to / decided / She / hasn't / what / do / still
_____

6 you / ruins / seen / Have / yet / the / ?
_____

7 homework / our / haven't / still / We / done
_____

4 ★★ **Complete the phone conversation. Use the verbs in the box and the adverbs in brackets.**

| visit Cambridge   be climbing |
| go   ~~be~~   not tidy   not tell   start |

Mum: Are you enjoying the summer camp?
Craig: Yes, but it's going really quickly! We ¹_'ve already been_ (already) here a week.
Mum: ²_____ (yet)?
Craig: Yes, I have – we've got a climbing wall here. And we ³_____ (already) sailing twice, and trekking!
Mum: Great! What other plans have you got?
Craig: Well, we ⁴_____ (yet). We're going on a guided tour of two university colleges, but the camp organiser ⁵_____ (still) us which day. OK, Mum, I've got to go. We all help around the camp site. I ⁶_____ (still) my things today! My group is cooking dinner and my friends ⁷_____ (already) in the kitchen.

5 ★★★ **Imagine you are on a school exchange to London. Write sentences about things you have and haven't done. Use *still*, *yet*, *already* and *just* and the ideas in the box.**

| ~~see Big Ben~~   meet my new teacher |
| go out with my new friends   buy new clothes |
| speak a lot of English   go into the city centre |

1 _I haven't seen Big Ben yet._

2 _____

3 _____

4 _____

5 _____

6 _____

Listening and vocabulary

Listening

1 ★ 🔊 **04** **Listen to a family from London talking about their holiday. Which sentence is true?**

a They are looking online at big hotels in lots of different countries.

b They are looking on an international house exchange website to find another family to exchange houses with.

c They find lots of holiday offers online but they all want to go to a different place.

2 ★★ 🔊 **04** **Listen again. Who is it? Write M for Mum, D for Dad, L for Laura and K for Kevin.**

1 _M_ has found lots of possible holiday places on a website.

2 ___ wants to go somewhere new for a change.

3 ___ suggests somewhere with water sports.

4 ___ doesn't want to go to a place with nothing to do in the evenings.

5 ___ likes an apartment in a city famous for art and culture.

6 ___ notices another family don't want a holiday in London.

7 ___ suggests going to another big city closer to London.

8 ___ has a friend who's been there and liked it.

9 ___ says he/she has wanted to go there for a long time.

10 ___ thinks they should email the family in Amsterdam.

Phrasal verbs (1)

3 ★ **Match the words in bold with one of the phrasal verbs in the box.**

> chill out   ~~pick up~~   come back
> look around   set off   find out

1 When my dad worked in Japan he tried to **learn** some Japanese from friends and neighbours.   _pick up_

2 I love Saturday afternoons, when I can **relax** with my friends.   _____

3 When we visit our village we always **start the journey** at six in the morning.   _____

4 My granny loves going on guided tours so she can **discover** the history of a place.   _____

5 After we arrived at the hotel, we went to **explore** the town.   _____

6 I always like the day we **return** from our holidays, because I see my friends again.   _____

4 ★★ **Complete the text with the phrasal verbs from Exercise 3.**

BORED?
NOTHING TO DO?

TRY OUR
DAY TRIP TO BRIGHTON!

We ¹ __set off__ from Victoria Station at 9.30 and ² _____ at 8 o'clock in the evening. There's lots of time to ³ _____ Brighton's many boutique shops. You can ⁴ _____ more about historical Brighton by going on our optional guided tour of the city centre, or maybe you prefer to ⁵ _____ at the beach. Learning English? You can ⁶ _____ more English here than in a classroom!

DON'T MISS IT!

Language focus 2

Present perfect with *for* and *since*

1 ★ **Complete the sentences in the box.**

> We can use the present perfect with *for* or *since* to talk about an action that started in the **¹**_____ and continues in the **²**_____ .
> Use **³**_____ with a period of time.
> Use **⁴**_____ with a specific date or time.

2 ★★ (Circle) **the correct options in the text.**

We haven't had a holiday in the mountains since **¹**(2010)/ three years. We had a tent then, but we've had this camper van since **²** last year / a year. My parents have wanted to go to the Alps for **³** three years ago / a long time, so this year we're in Switzerland. We've been here for **⁴** yesterday / five days, and it's rained every day since **⁵** then / five days. It hasn't been this wet on holiday since **⁶** three years / the time we went to England!

3 ★★ **Write present perfect sentences with the prompts. Use *for* or *since*.**

1 My grandparents / live / their flat / forty years
   My grandparents have lived in their flat for forty years.

2 We / not go / on holiday / six months
   _____

3 My sister / work / in Geneva / 2009
   _____

4 They / not visit us / a long time
   _____

5 I / not see / her / 2012
   _____

6 He / want / to go to Brazil / last year
   _____

Present perfect and past simple

4 ★★ **Complete the conversation with the correct tense of the verbs in brackets.**

A: **¹** *Have you ever been* (you go) on a school exchange?

B: Yes, I have. Last year I **²**_____ (go) to France.

A: Where **³**_____ (you go)?

B: Bordeaux. I **⁴**_____ (never see) such fantastic beaches.

A: What **⁵**_____ (you do) there?

B: We **⁶**_____ (go) sailing and surfing.

A: **⁷**_____ the French students _____ (come) here yet?

B: Yes, they're here now, in fact! They **⁸**_____ (be) here for a week.

A: So what **⁹**_____ (they do) so far?

B: Well, we **¹⁰**_____ (cook) them some traditional food, and they **¹¹**_____ (go) on a guided tour of the town.

5 ★★★ **Write a conversation about a trip. Use the one in Exercise 4 to help you. Use the present perfect and the past simple.**

A: Have you ever been to a summer camp?
B: Yes, I have. I went to one …

(Ex)plore interesting adjectives

6 ★★ **Complete the sentences with the adjectives in the box.**

> incredible   amazing   ~~spectacular~~
> important   perfect

1 The island has got high mountains and a volcano. The landscape is really __*spectacular*__ !

2 The mountains are amazing and it's the _____ place for climbing.

3 The view from the sea on the boat is absolutely _____ .

4 An _____ part of learning how to ski is learning how to fall!

5 Going on safari was the most _____ experience I've ever had.

Reading

1 ⭐ **Read the text about two holidays. What have they got in common?**

a They are both trekking holidays for families with teenagers.

b On both trips you stay in luxury hotels.

c Both holidays include a four-day trek in the mountains.

Bored with your holidays? Discover a new world with *Discovery*

Discovery has organised great holidays for 25 years, and we've just started holidays especially for families with teenagers. Our trips are carefully planned, and experienced, well-trained tour guides take groups of up to 15 people. *Porters* carry your *luggage*, so you can enjoy the *scenery*, and our cooks prepare delicious food every night.

Nepal Adventure Tour

Days 1–2 Chill out in Kathmandu, Nepal's capital city, where there are beautiful temples and monkeys climbing in the trees.

Days 3–10 The Annapurna Trek is spectacular, with amazing views of some of the world's highest mountains. We offer optional white-water rafting through the rapids. You sleep in *teahouses*, eat pancakes for breakfast and at dinner eat curry with your fingers, Nepalese style.

Days 11–12 The jungle of Chitwan National Park is a great place to relax after the trek. You can ride the elephants, and look for rare one-horned rhinos.

Days 13–14 Back to Kathmandu to shop for *souvenirs* in the bazaars.

Inca Trail For Teens

Days 1–3 Set off for Cusco, the ancient Inca capital. You can explore fascinating Inca ruins and look around this beautiful Spanish-style city. We also visit the colourful indigenous Pisac Market.

Day 4–5 We visit Misminay, where our Inca Trail porters live, to experience the traditional way of life of an Andean mountain village.

Days 6–7 Enjoy the *thrill* of white-water rafting or downhill mountain biking in the beautiful Sacred Valley.

Day 8–11 A four-day trek along the Inca Trail through spectacular scenery.

Day 12 Arrive at Machu Picchu and discover this ancient Inca citadel.

Days 13–14 Back to Cusco. Finish your holiday here shopping for souvenirs and chilling out.

2 ⭐⭐ **Complete the sentences with the words in *bold* from the text.**

1 I like travelling by train and looking out of the window at the _____ .

2 When I go on holiday, I always buy _____ to remind me of the places I've visited.

3 There's nothing like the _____ of a big rollercoaster – they are so exciting I always scream!

4 How much _____ have you got? You can only take 20 kilos on the plane.

5 In India the _____ are really hotel-restaurants, not cafés where you have a cup of tea.

6 The hotel _____ who carried our bags recommended a good restaurant.

3 ⭐⭐ **Read the text again. (Circle) the correct options.**

1 These holidays are especially for families with small children /(teenagers).

2 There **is / isn't** an experienced person leading the group on both holidays.

3 There are views of **high mountains / ancient cities** in Nepal.

4 You **see / don't see** wild animals on the Inca Trail.

5 You can go cycling **in Nepal / on the Inca Trail**.

6 You visit temples in **Kathmandu / Cusco**.

7 You can go shopping at the **beginning / end** of both trips.

8 You see where the porters live in **Chitwan National Park / Misminay**.

4 ⭐⭐⭐ **Read the sentences from postcards. Are they from Nepal or the Inca Trail? Write *N* or *I*.**

1 We're going to spend a few days chilling out in Cusco. Do you want anything?   *I*

2 Today we had a look around some ruins and went to a market.   ___

3 I've never ridden an elephant but it's a great way to see the jungle.   ___

4 We've been here for two days and we've seen some amazing temples.   ___

5 We went so fast on the bikes that I didn't have time to look at the scenery!   ___

6 The curries are delicious but I don't like eating with my fingers!   ___

5 ⭐⭐⭐ **Do you like this kind of holiday? Which of the two do you prefer and why? Write four or five sentences.**

Writing

A travel blog

1 Read Andy's travel blog. What kind of holiday is a *cruise*?

My holiday blog
a Mediterranean cruise

We've been here for six days and what
¹ _an amazing ship_ ! Since we left Barcelona,
I've been on the climbing wall and played
volleyball and mini-golf. There's also the
'Ocean Adventure Teen Club', with its
own swimming pool and activities. What
² _____ to make friends! I'd like
to stay on the ship all the time, but my parents
insist I see everywhere we visit.

We've already stopped in Nice, Florence and
Rome (what ³ _____ they have
in Italy!), and Athens – hot, crowded, and
what ⁴ _____ 😞. We visited the
island of Santorini yesterday, definitely my
favourite place – what ⁵ _____
! And we've just arrived at Mykonos. What
⁶ _____ they're having – I can
hear the music from here!

More soon …

Andy

Our ship – Voyager of the Seas

The Gang

2 Read the blog again. Complete the text with the words in the box.

> an incredible party   an amazing ship
> delicious ice creams   boring ruins
> beautiful beaches   a fantastic way

3 Read the blog again and answer the questions.

1 What kind of holiday is Andy having?
   He's having a cruise.

2 Where did it start?
   _____

3 What activities has he done on the ship?
   _____

4 What do his parents make him do?
   _____

5 How many places has he seen?
   _____

6 What did he like about Italy?
   _____

7 Why didn't he like Athens?
   _____

8 Which place does he like best so far?
   _____

4 Read the blog again. Tick (✓) the things in the list that Andy writes about.

where you started ☐
where you've been ☐
how long you've been on the trip ☐
what you've eaten ☐
what you've done ☐
what you've seen ☐
your favourite place ☐
your favourite activities ☐
how you feel about something ☐

Useful language Expressing how you feel, good or bad.

5 Complete the table with the adjectives in the box.

> awful   ~~incredible~~   amazing   disappointing
> boring   fantastic   ugly   spectacular   terrible

Good 😊	Bad 😞
incredible	

Writing

6 **Read the sentences and write how you felt. Use the words in Exercise 5 to help you.**

1 The Eiffel Tower was as good as we thought it would be.
   I thought it was fantastic.

2 I didn't think Hamburg was beautiful at all.
   _____

3 I almost fell asleep in the museum.
   _____

4 The food at the restaurant was disgusting.
   _____

5 There were tall mountains and beautiful lakes.
   _____

6 I couldn't believe it when I saw the tall buildings.
   _____

> **WRITING TIP**
> Make it better! ✓ ✓ ✓
> Use *What a/an* before singular countable nouns.
> Use *What* before singular uncountable and plural nouns.

7 **Rewrite the sentences with *What* or *What a/an*.**

1 It was a very exciting theme park.
   What an exciting theme park.

2 The fireworks were really spectacular.
   _____

3 The guided tour was very boring.
   _____

4 The landscape was incredible.
   _____

5 The souvenir shops were terrible.
   _____

8 **Rewrite the sentences. Put the word in brackets in the correct place.**

1 We've seen about 20 temples. (already)
   We've already seen about 20 temples.

2 I can't believe it was such a beautiful place. (still)
   _____

3 We haven't visited the museum. (yet)
   _____

4 They've gone skiing in the mountains. (just)
   _____

> **WRITING TIP**
> Make it better! ✓ ✓ ✓
> Use different ways to say 'my favourite ...'.

9 **Read the sentences. Which one does <u>not</u> mean *my favourite*?**

1 The safari has been the best thing *so far*.
2 *I've never eaten a better* ice cream.
3 The guided tour was *quite good*.
4 There is *no better way* to spend a summer.
5 *By far* the best activity has been the climbing.

10 **Read the blog again. Number the things in the list in the order they appear.**

Andy's favourite place ___
how long Andy has been on the trip _1_
what Andy has done ___
where Andy has been ___
where the trip started ___
how Andy feels about something ___

PLAN

11 **Imagine you are on a cruise. Use the list in Exercise 10 and your imagination to make notes.**

WRITE

12 **Write a travel blog post about your trip. Look at page 49 of the Student's Book to help you.**

_____
_____
_____
_____
_____
_____
_____
_____
_____
_____
_____
_____
_____
_____

CHECK

13 **Check your writing. Can you say YES to these questions?**

* Have you expressed how you feel – good and bad?
* Have you used sentences with *What a/an*?
* Are words like *still, already, yet* and *just* in the right place in the sentences?
* Have you used different ways to say *my favourite*?
* Are the spelling and punctuation correct?

Do you need to write a second draft?

Vocabulary
Expressions with *go*

1 **Match the trips with the places and things.**

1 go climbing   *d*
2 go on a safari   ___
3 go skiing   ___
4 go to a theme park   ___
5 go on a guided tour ___
6 go to summer camp   ___
7 go on a school exchange ___

a activities for young people
b historic buildings and museums
c roller coasters, rides, restaurants
d mountains
e a school in another country
f mountains and snow
g wild animals

Total: 6

Phrasal verbs (1)

2 **Use a word from each box to make phrasal verbs and complete the postcard.**

find chill pick come ~~look~~ set

out (x2) up ~~around~~ back off

Dear Lou,

We've had a fantastic time here in Berlin. We've had plenty of time to ¹___*look around*___ the city. It was fun to ²_____ about the city's history and culture, and we also managed to ³_____ some German! There are a lot of cafés to eat ice cream and ⁴_____ . Tonight we have to go to bed early because we have to ⁵_____ at 6 am tomorrow morning. Our holiday is over and it's time to ⁶_____ home!

Annie

Total: 5

Language focus
Present perfect with *still*, *yet*, *already* and *just*

3 **Circle the correct options to complete each mini-conversation.**

1 **A:** Has your sister left for London **yet** / still?
  B: Yes, she left yesterday but she **already** / **still** hasn't phoned us.
2 **A:** Have you booked your hotel **still** / **yet**?
  B: No, I **already** / **still** haven't decided which one I prefer.
3 **A:** Have you seen Buckingham Palace **still** / **yet**?
  B: No, but we've **still** / **already** seen some great museums and art galleries.
4 **A:** Why is your hair wet?
  B: I've **just** / **still** come back from swimming.

Total: 6

Present perfect with *for* and *since*

4 **Circle the correct options.**

1 I've lived here **for** / **since** January.
2 Suzanne has played the guitar **for** / **since** a very long time.
3 We've been friends **for** / **since** we were little children.
4 I haven't seen you **for** / **since** ages.
5 Mark has had his car **for** / **since** five years.
6 They haven't visited us **for** / **since** last year.

Total: 5

Present perfect and past simple

5 **Complete the mini-conversations with the correct tense of the verbs in brackets.**

1 **A:** *Have you ever been* (you ever go) to Italy?
  B: Yes, we _____ (go) there last summer.
2 **A:** I _____ (eat) some octopus yesterday.
  B: Really? I _____ (never eat) octopus.
3 **A:** _____ (you see) this film?
  B: Yes, I _____ (see) it twice.

Total: 5

Language builder

6 Complete the email with the missing words. Circle the correct options.

1	**a** ever	**b** never	**c** yet
2	**a** always go	**b** always are going	**c** go always
3	**a** go	**b** 've been	**c** went
4	**a** were taking	**b** 've taken	**c** take
5	**a** comes	**b** came	**c** was coming
6	**a** don't take usually	**b** usually don't take	**c** don't usually take
7	**a** take	**b** 'm taking	**c** was taking
8	**a** should	**b** have	**c** shouldn't
9	**a** have	**b** 've to	**c** should
10	**a** you doing	**b** you are doing	**c** are you doing
11	**a** You have to	**b** You do have to	**c** Do you have to

Total: 10

Hi Bruno,

This is the first day of our trip to Switzerland. I've ¹___ been to Switzerland before. The mountains are really amazing! I'm here with my parents and my best friend, Susan. We ²___ on holiday together every year. Yesterday, we ³___ hiking in the forest. When we ⁴___ pictures of some flowers, a small goat ⁵___ up to us and started eating them! I ⁶___ a lot of photos, but this year I ⁷___ a lot because I want to make a photo blog when I get back home. I ⁸___ stop writing now because I ⁹___ to get up early tomorrow. What ¹⁰___ this summer? ¹¹___ do any schoolwork?

Write soon,

Janey

Vocabulary builder

7 Circle the correct options.

1 Going on a ___ is a great way to meet students from other countries.
 a safari **b** school exchange **c** guided tour

2 While I was in Poland I ___ a few words of Polish.
 a set up **b** showed up **c** picked up

3 It was boiling for about three days and then the ___ went away.
 a snowstorm **b** heat wave **c** lightning

4 We looked at the ___ but we didn't know where we were.
 a map **b** compass **c** torch

5 Sarah hasn't ___ the photos online yet.
 a hung **b** given **c** posted

6 I haven't had much time ___ myself yet. I've been very busy.
 a on **b** by **c** with

7 Can you set ___ the drums before we start playing?
 a on **b** down **c** up

8 We went on a ___ tour of the castle and gardens.
 a guiding **b** guided **c** guide

9 You have to blow very hard to make a sound on the ___ .
 a trumpet **b** piano **c** banjo

10 I'm hungry because I haven't even ___ a snack today.
 a had **b** taken **c** done

Total: 9

Speaking

8 Put the words in the correct order to make questions for signing up for an activity.

1 about / What / then / food, / ?
 What about food, then?

2 trip / long / How / is / the / ?
 _____

3 include / the price / Does / food / ?
 _____

4 bring / need / I / do / What / to / ?
 _____

5 a few / Can / about / I / you / the trip things / ask / ?
 _____

6 only / it / for / experienced / climbers / Is / ?
 _____

Total: 5

Total: 51

Present perfect with *still*, *yet*, *already* and *just*

Remember that:
- we put *still* directly after the subject
  ✓ *I still haven't adjusted to life at sea.*
  ✗ *I ~~haven't adjusted to life at sea still.~~*
- we put *yet* after the complete verb phrase
  ✓ *Have you brushed your teeth yet?*
  ✗ *Have you brushed ~~yet your teeth?~~*
- we normally put *just* and *already* between *have* and the past participle
  ✓ *I've already packed my swimming costume.*
  ✗ *I've ~~packed already~~ my swimming costume.*
  ✓ *I have just climbed up and down the mast.*
  ✗ *I ~~just have~~ climbed up and down the mast.*

1 **Are the sentences correct? Correct the incorrect sentences.**

1 I just have returned from my climbing trip.
   I have just returned from my climbing trip.

2 I haven't still tried skiing, but I'm sure I'll enjoy it.

3 I haven't been yet there, but I really want to go.

4 She has made already a lot of friends on the adventure holiday.

5 They just have bought tickets for a guided tour of the city.

6 My sister is five, so she yet hasn't been sailing.

7 I have just received a letter from my grandfather.

8 He said he would call me, but I still haven't heard from him.

Present perfect with *for* and *since*

Remember that:
- we use *for* with periods of time
  ✓ *We've been on the road in our camper van for ten days.*
  ✗ *We've been on the road in our camper van ~~since ten days.~~*
- we use *since* with a specific date, time or event
  ✓ *We haven't had anything to eat since lunchtime.*
  ✗ *We haven't had anything to eat ~~for lunchtime.~~*

2 **Circle the correct words.**

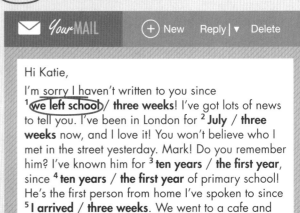

✉ *Your*MAIL   ⊕ New   Reply | ▼   Delete

Hi Katie,

I'm sorry I haven't written to you since ¹**we left school**/ **three weeks**! I've got lots of news to tell you. I've been in London for ²**July** / **three weeks** now, and I love it! You won't believe who I met in the street yesterday. Mark! Do you remember him? I've known him for ³**ten years** / **the first year**, since ⁴**ten years** / **the first year** of primary school! He's the first person from home I've spoken to since ⁵**I arrived** / **three weeks**. We went to a cafe and we talked for ⁶**hours** / **six o'clock**! He has visited ten towns in England since ⁷**six weeks** / **June**. What an adventure!

I'll write again soon.

Love,

Lara

Expressions with *go*

Remember that:
- we use *go* + *–ing* to talk about doing an activity. We never use a preposition between *go* and the activity.
  ✓ *Did you go climbing?*
  ✗ *Did you go ~~for~~ climbing?*
  ✗ *Did you go ~~to~~ climbing?*

3 **Find and correct four more mistakes with *go* in the poster.**

Adventures to go!

With *Adventures to go!* you can go ~~to~~ climbing in the mountains or for trekking in the forest. If you like water sports, you can go sailing on a clear blue lake, or go to swimming in the sea. Why not go to camping for a few days? Or, if you like, you can go to a hotel instead. If you're feeling tired from all these activities, you can go on a guided bus tour or go to a safari park for the day. And there's even a bus to the city every day for those who want to go to shopping. The fun never stops with *Adventures to go!*

www.adventures2go.net

5 Let's talk

Vocabulary

Communication

1 ★ **Match the words and phrases with the correct definitions.**

1 the name of a post on Twitter _____d____

2 something you write, send and receive on your mobile phone _____

3 something you write, send and receive on your computer or on the Internet _____

4 to speak informally to someone face-to-face _____

5 a place for online discussion with lots of people _____

6 to speak to (and see) someone computer to computer _____

7 a personal website that gives regular information to readers _____

8 a website that allows users to communicate with each other by posting information, photos and messages _____

9 a short message on a social network site _____

a email   f post
b chat   g forum
c text message   h Skype™
d Tweet   i social network
e blog

2 ★ **Write communication words from Exercise 1 next to the correct definitions.**

1 the name of a post on Twitter _____Tweet_____

2 something you write, send and receive on your mobile phone _____

3 speaking informally to someone face to face _____

4 a place for online discussion with lots of people _____

5 speak to (and see) someone computer to computer _____

6 a website that gives readers regular information _____

3 ★★ **Complete the text about how Josh's brother communicates.**

My brother is a university student but he doesn't study much. When he gets up he goes on Twitter to read all the [1] __Tweets__ from people he follows. After breakfast he writes a(n) [2]_____ – he usually talks about university life. He reads all the [3]_____ he's got on Facebook. Then he reads and answers any [4]_____ too, but he says a lot of them are junk with adverts for things he's not interested in. He also spends time on a skateboard [5]_____ talking to skaters from all over the world. In the evening we often talk on [6]_____ (he helps me with my homework!). When he goes out with his friends, they use WhatsApp and organise it by [7]_____ . So my brother does a lot of communicating. The funny thing is, he's got a mobile phone and a home phone, but he never makes any [8]_____ !

4 ★★★ **How do you and your friends communicate? Answer the questions and write at least five sentences.**

1 Which ways to communicate are the most popular with you and your friends? Why?

2 Did you use the same ones last year? Why?/Why not?

3 Are there any you never use? Why not?

4 How do your parents and grandparents communicate? Is it the same as you?

I usually use text messages on my mobile to talk to my friends because ...

Language focus 1

will, might, may + adverbs of possibility

1 ★ Circle the correct words in the table.

1	Use *will* to show we are **sure / not sure** about the future.
2	Use *might* to show we are **sure / not sure** about the future.
3	The negative of *will* is **don't will / won't**
4	The negative of *might* is **don't might / might not**.
5	Use *will* or *might* + **infinitive / -ing** form.

2 ★★ Complete the sentences with the correct form of *will* or *might*.

1 I'm not sure, but my parents ____*might*____ give me a smartphone for my birthday.

2 He's not answering his email. He _____ be on holiday. I don't know.

3 There _____ be enough time to discuss it in class, so let's talk about it on the forum.

4 She _____ be able to phone you. I don't know if her mobile works there.

5 I'm sure Amy _____ post the photos on Facebook so that we can all see them.

3 ★★ Read the rules. Are they true (*T*) or false (*F*)?

1 We use *definitely* and *certainly* when we are very sure of the future. _T_

2 When we are less sure of the future, we use *probably*. ___

3 We can't use these adverbs with negative verbs. ___

4 We can use these adverbs with *might (not)*. ___

5 With affirmative verbs the adverb goes before *will*. ___

6 With negative verbs the adverb goes before *won't*. ___

4 ★★★ Complete the email about Gina's plans. Use the verbs in the box with *might* or *will*, and the adverbs in brackets.

> ~~visit~~ not come   not have to   not be
> agree   stay   have   be

Hi Jo,

How are things? I've got some great news! Keira and I ¹ _will definitely visit_ (definitely) our grandparents in July. We ² _____ (certainly) for three weeks, and maybe longer if we can. ³ _____ you _____ there in July? I hope so! My dad ⁴ _____ (definitely) with us because he's working, but Mum ⁵ _____ work all of July and so maybe she can join us later.

The other news is that I ⁶ _____ a party for my birthday. Dad has said yes but Mum hasn't decided yet. It's OK, I think she ⁷ _____ (probably) soon! If I do have one, can you come? You can stay the weekend. Please say yes! It ⁸ _____ (certainly) the same without you!

Gina

5 ★★★ Write at least five sentences about you and your life. Use *will*, *might* and adverbs of probability and possibility. Use the ideas in the box or your own ideas.

> play a (sport) match   go to the cinema   go swimming
> spend a day at the beach   visit my grandparents
> buy a new game

I might go swimming with my friends on Saturday.

Explore communications collocations

6 ★★ Circle the correct options.

1 A lot of my virtual / **computer** friends are also friends in real life.

2 I try not to look at **social / friend** network sites when I'm doing my homework.

3 My last status **update / post** just said 'Help!' – I was doing my homework!

4 My dad says we are the **digital / network** generation because we don't know a world without computers.

5 Sometimes it's better to talk **face- / head-** to-face than online.

Listening and vocabulary

Listening

1 ★ 🔊 05 **Listen to Olga and Tanya discussing something Tanya has done. Which sentence is true?**

  a Tanya has stopped using Facebook for a month.
  b Tanya has decided never to use Facebook again.
  c Tanya has received a lot of insulting Tweets.

2 ★★ 🔊 05 **Read the sentences. Listen again and circle the correct options.**

  1 Olga tried to go on Tanya's Facebook page to **say happy birthday** / **post a website link**.
  2 Tanya thinks she **should** / **shouldn't** spend less time on Facebook.
  3 Tanya wants to spend more time socialising with her **school friends** / **real friends**.
  4 Tanya thinks that some of the posts she reads are **private** / **not true**.
  5 A friend of Olga's **sent insults** / **received insults** on Twitter.
  6 Olga doesn't think Tanya needs to **stop using Facebook** / **use Facebook any more**.
  7 Tanya is worried about people seeing **her private details** / **her friends' Facebook pages**.
  8 Tanya plans to spend more time **chatting to her friends** / **using different social networks**.
  9 Tanya is **sure** / **not sure** what she's going to do at the end of her experiment.
  10 Olga is going to contact Tanya on **Facebook** / **Skype™** later.

Communication verbs

3 ★ **Write the verbs in the box next to the correct definitions.**

> whisper complain boast gossip
> ~~argue~~ joke shout criticise

  1 disagree with someone, sometimes loudly or aggressively   _argue_
  2 say how good you are at doing something   _____
  3 say something funny   _____
  4 talk very quietly so other people can't hear   _____
  5 talk very loudly   _____
  6 talk about other people   _____
  7 say negative things about someone   _____
  8 say that you don't like something   _____

4 ★★ **Complete the text with the correct form of the verbs in Exercise 3.**

I've got a great group of friends I've known since primary school. We always meet at the weekend to laugh and ¹___*joke*___ , and ²_____ about people we know. My friends never ³_____ me for what I wear or ⁴_____ about me in front of me. They like me for who I am. We know each other well, too. Alicia ⁵_____ that she's the best basketball player in the school, and Nuria and I ⁶_____ that our parents are too strict. Sometimes we ⁷_____ about where to meet and what to do, but we never get angry or ⁸_____ and we always agree in the end.

Language focus 2

First conditional + *may/might, be able to*

1 ★ **Match the sentence halves.**

1	If you phone me tonight,	_b_
2	If we start a class blog,	___
3	She may not stay on Twitter	___
4	If you post the photos on Facebook,	___
5	Will you send me the stuff by email	___
6	I won't know their address	___

a   if you have time?
b   I might not have time to talk to you.
c   everyone will be able to see them.
d   will everyone post on it?
e   if they don't text me.
f   if people insult her.

2 ★★ **Put the verbs in brackets in the correct form to complete this chain of events. Use the verb prompts in brackets to help you.**

Now the problem is … If I ¹_____*put*_____ (put) my party on Facebook, all my friends ²_____ (see) it – and I've got 217! If everyone ³_____ (see) it, they ⁴_____ (might/think) it's an open invitation. If they ⁵_____ (think) it's an open invitation, they ⁶_____ (may/invite) more people. And if they ⁷_____ (invite) more people, everyone ⁸_____ (might/decide) to come and I ⁹_____ (not/have) enough room for them. If too many people ¹⁰_____ (come), they ¹¹_____ (may/break) things. And if they ¹²_____ (break) things and my parents ¹³_____ (find out), I ¹⁴_____ (not/be able to) have any more parties!

3 ★★ **Complete the conversation with the correct form of the verbs in the box. Use *may* or *might* when the person is not sure.**

~~know~~ talk whisper think be
~~ask~~ give tell hear not buy

Tim: What shall we get Dad for his birthday? He's 40!
Sara: No idea. Let's ask him.
Tim: No, if we ¹_*ask*_ him, he ²____*will know*____ what his present is. That's boring. If we ³_____ him a surprise, I don't know – it ⁴_____ more fun!
Sara: Yes, but if he ⁵_____ us, we ⁶_____ him something he doesn't like.
Tim: Well, we could ask Mum, she'll know!
Sara: OK, good idea! If you ⁷_____ to her now, I don't think Dad ⁸_____ you. But whisper!
Tim: Don't be silly! If I ⁹_____ , he ¹⁰_____ something mysterious is going on, don't you think?

4 ★★★ **Write a chain of events like the one in Exercise 3. Use one of the ideas below or your own idea. How long can you make the chain?**

If I finish my homework quickly, …
If my parents allow me to …
If I lose my mobile phone, …

Explore phrasal verbs (2)

5 ★★ **Match the sentence halves.**

1	Do you think this app will	_e_
2	English is very flexible so we keep on adding	___
3	Does anyone know when social networks	___
4	The number of people on social network sites	___
5	I speak German so when we went to Berlin	___

a   is going up every year.
b   I was able to get by.
c   new words to the language.
d   started coming into use?
e   turn into the next popular thing?

Reading

1 ★ **Read the text about Tony Anderson. How has the Internet changed his life?**

BREAKING DOWN
THE BARRIERS!

Tony Anderson is 15 and, like most people his age, he spends a lot of time on his computer and smartphone, but his parents aren't complaining. In fact, they're pleased. This is because Tony was born *deaf*, but now, thanks to technology and social media, his life has completely changed. Young deaf people have attended the same schools as other children for a long time, but in the past they found it difficult to make friends. Most deaf people could only communicate using sign language, and so their classmates couldn't talk to them. And if you can't communicate, you won't be able to *take part* in social activities with other teenagers. So deaf teenagers felt *isolated* and bored, didn't have a social life, and often suffered from low self-esteem.

Then along came the technological revolution, with computers, the Internet and mobile phones. Teenagers began to communicate more and more by text message and go on social media sites like Facebook and Twitter. For deaf teenagers, the Internet is an ideal way to communicate, because it doesn't need hearing or speaking. More importantly, everyone uses it, not just deaf people. As Tony explains, 'Now, if you're a deaf teenager, no-one will know you're different. It's incredible! I can post on chat forums or social networks and the other people probably won't know I'm deaf, so they *treat* me like everyone else. It's made me a lot more relaxed and confident.'

The other thing Tony enjoys is being able to connect up with other teenagers who are deaf. 'We've all had similar experiences in life, so we understand each other. I've made some good friends online, and sometimes we *meet up*, too. One day soon, deaf teenagers might be able to have a totally normal social life because of the Internet!'

2 ★★ **Complete the sentences with the words in *bold* from the text.**

1 Let's _____ tomorrow morning and go to the comic exhibition.
2 Would you like to _____ in an experiment?
3 Mark was ill when he was a baby and now he is _____ in one ear.
4 You mustn't _____ your brother like that! Be nice to him.
5 We lived in a remote place and I felt very _____ .

3 ★★ **Read the text again and circle the correct options.**

1 Why does Tony spend a lot of time on his computer?
   a He's a typical teenager.
   b He doesn't do any school work.
   c He hasn't got a mobile phone.
2 Why were deaf teenagers often unhappy before the Internet?
   a Schools didn't know how to teach them.
   b They didn't have any friends.
   c It was difficult to communicate with others.
3 What was <u>not</u> true for deaf teenagers before technology?
   a They didn't often go out with friends.
   b A lot of them didn't have much confidence.
   c They all had to communicate with sign language.
4 Why is technology so important for Tony?
   a It means he's like other teenagers.
   b He's good at it because he's deaf.
   c He can explain to people that he's deaf.
5 What is <u>not</u> true about Tony's life nowadays?
   a He's got a normal social life.
   b He doesn't know any other deaf teenagers.
   c He feels better about himself.

4 ★★★ **Read the summary of the text. Correct five mistakes.**

Tony Anderson is a deaf teenager who uses the Internet and social networks to make friends and ¹<u>to go to school</u>. His parents ²<u>are worried</u> about him spending a lot of time on the Internet because it has helped Tony in his social life and ³<u>in sports</u>. Now with the Internet and mobile phones people ⁴<u>still know he's deaf</u> and he can communicate with other people. He's made a lot of friends and some of his new friends are deaf. ⁵<u>He'd like to meet up</u> with them.

1 _____*have a social life*_____
2 _____
3 _____
4 _____
5 _____

5 ★★★ **Tony's story shows a positive aspect of the Internet. What other good things are there? Write at least three more advantages.**

The Internet helps young people in different cities or countries communicate.

Writing

An essay

1 Read Harry's essay. Does he agree or disagree with the essay title?

TEENAGERS USE SOCIAL MEDIA SITES TOO MUCH. DISCUSS.

A Thousands of teenagers post on social networks every day. In fact, it has become the most popular way for them to communicate. Why is it so popular, and do we use it too much?

B [1] _____Firstly_____ , social networks are a quick, easy and cheap way to tell your friends your news. You can [2]_____ post photos and weblinks, and share music and video clips. [3]_____ , you can combine it with other computer activities.

C [4]_____ there are negatives, too. [5]_____ , a lot of 'friends' aren't friends at all. If you aren't careful, you'll share personal information with complete strangers. [6]_____ , some people might only socialise online.

D On balance, I don't think teenagers use these sites too much, and we still meet our friends face to face.

2 Complete Harry's essay about social media. Use the words in the box.

> ~~firstly~~   lastly   also   for one thing   in addition   on the other hand

3 Read the essay again. Complete the notes in the table.

Facts to introduce the topic		Positive arguments	
1 _thousands of teenagers_ post on social networks every day		3 quick, easy and _____	
2 has become the most popular way _____		4 _____ photos and links, _____ music and video clips	
		5 _____ it with other computer activities	
Negative arguments		**Harry's opinion and why**	
6 some _____ aren't friends at all		9 teens _____ these sites too much	
7 you should be _____ with personal information		10 still meet _____	
8 some people might only _____			

Useful language Introducing points and arguments

4 Complete the table with the words in the box and the words in Exercise 2.

> ~~however~~   nevertheless   what's more   on one hand

Ordering points	Adding points	Introducing arguments	Contrasting arguments
			however

Writing

5 **Put the words in order to make essay introduction questions.**

1 places / Are / social / dangerous / networks / ?
Are social networks dangerous places?

2 age / you / Should / everyone / your / tell / ?
_____

3 safe / information / share / Is / to / it / personal / ?
_____

4 it / a / photos / social / idea / to / network / post / Is / good / on / a / ?
_____

> **WRITING TIP**
> **Make it better! ✓ ✓ ✓**
> It's always better to make sure general statements don't mean *everyone*, *everything* or *always*.

6 **Put the words in brackets in the correct place in the general statements.**

1 Teenagers should ⌃avoid putting photos of *generally* themselves on the Internet. (generally)

2 People share all sorts of information on social networks. (may)

3 We shouldn't post any information about ourselves online. (perhaps)

4 Other people find out all about you from your Facebook profile. (can)

> **WRITING TIP**
> **Make it better! ✓ ✓ ✓**
> Give your own opinion and use different expressions.

7 **Read the sentences. Which one does <u>not</u> give an opinion?**

1 I don't really think people know about the dangers of Facebook.

2 In my view, it is very dangerous to put personal information on social network sites.

3 There have been many stories of people using other people's personal information online.

4 In my opinion, social networking sites are not safe.

5 I believe it's good to learn how to use these sites.

8 **When you write an essay you should include four paragraphs. Complete the sentences with the words in the box.**

> against   conclusion   ~~introduction~~
> opinion   favour

1 Paragraph A is the ___*introduction*___ .
2 Paragraph B gives arguments in _____ .
3 Paragraph C gives arguments _____ .
4 Paragraph D gives the _____ , including your _____ .

PLAN

9 **You are going to write an essay with the title: 'It is dangerous to put too much personal information on social networking sites. Discuss.' Use the paragraphs in Exercise 8 and your own ideas to make notes.**

WRITE

10 **Write your essay. Look at page 61 of the Student's Book to help you.**

_____
_____
_____
_____
_____
_____
_____
_____
_____
_____
_____
_____
_____
_____
_____

CHECK

11 **Check your writing. Can you say YES to these questions?**

• Have you included all the paragraphs in Exercise 8?
• Have you introduced your points and arguments?
• Have you used a question in the introduction?
• Have you made sure general statements don't mean *everyone*, *everything* or *always*?
• Have you given your own opinion?
• Are the spelling and punctuation correct?

Do you need to write a second draft?

Vocabulary
Communication

1 Are these sentences true (T) or false (F)?

1 You can send photos and documents by email. _T_
2 You can join a discussion group on a forum. ___
3 You can send Tweets to a large group of people on Twitter. ___
4 You can speak and listen to someone with text messages. ___
5 You can write a blog post to tell other people about your life. ___
6 You can have a live chat with someone on a forum. ___

Total: 5

Communication verbs

2 Complete the sentences with the words in the box.

boast   argue   ~~whisper~~   complain   joke   shout

1 Don't talk so loudly – you should always __whisper__ in the library.
2 I don't want to _____ , but I'm very good at repairing computers.
3 We shouldn't _____ about the food. At least it's not very expensive.
4 They tried to _____ about it, but he was really upset and didn't laugh.
5 There's no need to _____ – I can hear you very well!
6 I know we disagree sometimes, but I don't want to _____ .

Total: 5

Language focus
will, may, might + adverbs of possibility

3 Match the sentence halves.

1 Everyone will definitely _d_
2 Our parents might not ___
3 How might the world be different ___
4 I'll probably Skype™ you later ___
5 Social networks certainly won't replace ___
6 Will you write ___

a to talk about the party.
b face-to-face communications.
c ever understand Facebook.
d use social media in the future.
e blog posts on holiday?
f in 50 years' time?

Total: 5

First conditional + may/might, be able to

4 Complete the first conditional sentences with the correct form of the verbs in brackets. Use may or might when the person is not sure.

1 If you _____give_____ (give) me your email address, I'll _____send_____ (send) you an email about the party.
2 I think she _____ (be) very upset if I _____ (not reply) to her email.
3 If I _____ (invite) everyone on Facebook, there _____ (be) too many people.
4 _____ (you send) me a text message if you _____ (get) home late?
5 It's possible he _____ (get) a better job if he _____ (learn) more about computers.
6 If you _____ (work) harder at home, you _____ (not have) the same problems in class. I'm not sure though.

Total: 5

Language builder

5 Complete the conversation with the missing words. Circle the correct options.

Dave: What ¹___ just now?
Tom: I ²___ my text messages.
Dave: How often ³___ check your messages?
Tom: Once or twice an hour. My mum ⁴___ me a message about helping her to wash the car this afternoon.
Dave: I hate having to help around the house! Do you think robots ⁵___ do all our work for us in the future?
Tom: I'm not sure. I think we ⁶___ robots in hospitals and maybe in schools.
Dave: If we ⁷___ robots in schools, we ⁸___ need teachers any more.
Tom: I'm not sure about that. We ⁹___ teachers, but we ¹⁰___ talk to them on Skype™.

1	a	you were doing	**b**	were you doing	c	you doing
2	a	was checking	b	'm checking	c	check
3	a	do usually you	b	usually do you	c	do you usually
4	a	just has sent	b	has just sent	c	has sent just
5	a	will	b	won't	c	are
6	a	'll certainly have	b	certainly will have	c	'll have certainly
7	a	have	b	'll have	c	'd have
8	a	will	b	might not	c	don't
9	a	'll definitely need	b	might need definitely	c	definitely might need
10	a	might have	b	might have to	c	have to

Total: 9

Vocabulary builder

6 Circle the correct options.

1 Sometimes it's better to talk face-___-face.
   a on   b by   **c** to
2 Abby sent a very funny text ___ last night. Look.
   a network   b post   c message
3 Eva posted a photo of the ___ park on Facebook.
   a theme   b summer   c guided
4 Don't worry, it's not true. I'm only ___ !
   a gossiping   b joking   c whispering
5 Could you please ___ your bedroom? It's a mess.
   a pick up   b set up   c tidy up
6 I'm going ___ for clothes tomorrow.
   a shopping   b getting   c buying
7 Have you seen the new ___ on our school wall?
   a sculpture   b paint   c mural
8 Stop ___ . I can hear you in my bedroom!
   a boasting   b arguing   c shouting
9 The number of students in our school has ___ in the last few years.
   a gone up   b kept on   c shown up
10 I'd like to relax and ___ at the beach for a few hours.
   a pick up   b get by   c chill out

Total: 9

Speaking

7 Put the sentences in the correct order to make a conversation.

___ **Lynn:** Listen, I think I can help you. Let's practise some test questions together.
___ **Lynn:** Don't worry! Of course you will!
_1_ **Lynn:** What's the matter Sally? You look worried.
___ **Lynn:** No, you're not. It'll turn out all right.
___ **Sally:** I've got a test tomorrow and I'm really worried I won't pass.
___ **Sally:** I don't think it will. It never does.
___ **Sally:** OK! That sounds like a good idea.
___ **Sally:** You know I'm really bad at Maths.

Total: 7

Total: 45

will, might/may + adverbs of possibility

1 Circle the correct options.

During my trip to London …

1 I might **going** / **go** / **went** to an art gallery.
2 I will **visited** / **visiting** / **visit** my uncle.
3 I might **sent** / **send** / **sending** some postcards.
4 I will **buying** / **buy** / **bought** some souvenirs.
5 I might **take** / **taking** / **took** a boat trip.
6 I will **phoning** / **phone** / **phoned** my parents every day.

First conditional

> Remember that:
> - we use *if* + subject + the present simple in the action/situation clause
>   ✓ *If I'm late, I will send you a text.*
> - we use *will/won't* + infinitive to talk about the consequences of the action/situation
>   ✓ *If I'm late, I will send you a text.*
>   ✗ *If I am late, I send you a text.*
> - We don't use *will/won't* in the same clause as *if*.
>   ✓ *If I'm late, I will send you a text.*
>   ✗ *If I will be late, I will send you a text.*

2 Complete the sentences with the correct form of the verb in brackets and *will* if needed.

1 If I ____find____ (find) the information, I ____will call____ (call) you.
2 If I _____ (have) time, I _____ (come) to see you on Saturday.
3 I _____ (meet) you after school if you _____ (want) me to.
4 If Lara _____ (be) ill, we _____ (not go) to the cinema tonight.
5 You _____ (not pass) your exams if you _____ (not work) hard.

at the moment/in the future

> Remember that:
> - we use *in the future* to talk about what will happen in a period of time that is to come
>   ✓ *Tablets will be popular in the future.*
>   ✗ *Tablets will be popular at the future.*
> - we use *at the moment* to talk about what is happening now
>   ✓ *Smartphones are popular at the moment.*
>   ✗ *Smartphones are popular at moment.*

3 Find and correct four more mistakes with *at the moment/in the future* in the text.

> **Marcus:** Hi Helen, what are you studying ~~in~~ *at* the moment?
> **Helen:** I'm reading about social networks for a school project.
> **Marcus:** That's interesting. Do you use any social networks?
> **Helen:** Well, at moment, I only use them to keep in contact with my cousins. But a lot of my friends use Facebook now, so I might use it more on the future. What about you?
> **Marcus:** Oh, I'm not on any social networks on the moment, but I think the future it will be important for my job.

complain

> Remember that:
> - the infinitive of the verb is *complain*; the *-ing* form is *complaining*, and the past simple is *complained*
>   ✓ *He complained about the noise in the classroom.*
>   ✗ *He complaint about the noise in the classroom.*
> - we use *about* after *complain* to talk about things we do not like
>   ✓ *He complained about the noise in the classroom.*
>   ✗ *He complained for the noise in the classroom.*
>   ✗ *He complained with the noise in the classroom.*

4 Are the sentences correct? Correct the incorrect sentences.

1 When was the last time you complaint for something?
   When was the last time you complained about something?
2 Jane is always complaining about her sister.
   _____
3 You shouldn't have complainted! Now they'll be angry.
   _____
4 My parents complain about the time I spend on Facebook.
   _____
5 I don't know what you're complaining with. It's great here!
   _____
6 They complaint for the homework, but the teacher didn't listen.
   _____

Fears

Vocabulary

Fears

1 ★ **Put the letters in order to make eight fears. Then write them under the correct pictures.**

> bdirs   flist   het adkr   ceinsst
> fgilny   aeknss   eghhist   cwnsol

1 _____flying_____

2 _____

3 _____

4 _____

5 _____

6 _____

7 _____

8 _____

2 ★★ **Complete the sentences with the fears from Exercise 1.**

1 Tobey Maguire, the Spider-Man actor, is afraid of _heights_ and tall buildings!

2 The Malayan Blue Krait is one of the most venomous _____ in the world.

3 City people often complain that the _____ sing too loudly in the country.

4 To get to the top of the Empire State Building you have to take two _____ . They aren't quick – the total time is 1½ minutes.

5 Mosquitoes are the most dangerous _____ in the world as they carry malaria.

6 According to statistics, _____ is safer than driving or going by coach.

7 The organisation '_____ without Borders' makes people in difficult situations laugh.

8 At night, when you are in _____ , noises sound a lot louder than during the day.

3 ★★ **Complete the text about an awful holiday.**

What a holiday! My dad is terrified of [1] _flying_ so we went to Spain on a coach – 33 hours! The hotel was great, but we were on the fourteenth floor. My mum refused to go in the [2] _____ as she's claustrophobic. Luckily the hotel moved us to the second floor and she used the stairs. I had to share a room with my brother. He's scared of [3] _____ so he slept with the lights on, but I couldn't go to sleep. Then the [4] _____ outside woke me up at five every morning! One day, on a guided tour, we had to walk up a mountain path. My dad really doesn't like [5] _____ and didn't go up, and my mum decided she heard [6] _____ moving in the grass and went back down. We had a picnic lunch but there were tiny flying [7] _____ everywhere. It was horrible! At least the [8] _____ at the circus made everyone laugh. No-one in my family is afraid of them!

4 ★★★ **Can you imagine why people are afraid of these things? Write at least five sentences. Use the ideas in the box or your own ideas.**

> they bite   they move fast   you could fall
> you could crash   dangerous   they attack
> imagine monsters   wear a strange costume

People are afraid of insects because they bite and have got a lot of legs.

Language focus 1

be going to / will / Present continuous

1 ★ (Circle) the correct words.

  1 Use **will / going to / the present continuous** for personal intentions.

  2 Use **will / going to / the present continuous** for predictions.

  3 Use **will / going to / the present continuous** for definite arrangements.

2 ★★ Write sentences about the future. Use *will, going to* or the present continuous.

  1 I / visit / my cousin / in July (definite arrangement)
    I'm going to visit my cousin in July. _____

  2 This social network / be / very popular / with teenagers (prediction)
    _____

  3 Hugh / sing / a song / at the school concert (definite arrangement)
    _____

  4 My dad / definitely / not / pick up the spider (prediction)
    _____

  5 I / complain / to the director about the lifts (intention)
    _____

  6 Harry / post / a Tweet / about the judo competition (intention)
    _____

3 ★★ Complete the conversation with a future form of the verbs in the box or a short answer.

> be can ~~spend~~ go (x2) not go
> write leave take

  A: Where ¹ *are you going to spend* Easter?
  B: Karin and I ² _____ on an adventure holiday.
  A: Fantastic! What activities are there?
  B: Oh, lots! Look, here's the information. But I ³ _____ rock climbing. I hate heights.
  A: Oh, wow! There's sailing! ⁴ _____ sailing?
  B: No, I ⁵ _____ . I can't swim and we ⁶ _____ too busy with the other activities!
  A: So when ⁷ _____ ?
  B: We ⁸ _____ the bus on Friday evening.
  A: Well, send us some photos.
  B: I don't think we ⁹ _____ post photos – there's no Internet! But I ¹⁰ _____ a blog post about it when I get back.

4 ★★ Complete the text with the correct future form of the verbs in brackets.

I've just finished talking to the doctor about my snake phobia. He says he ¹ *'ll be able to* (can) help me. Did I tell you that I ² _____ (go) on holiday to the Amazon in the summer? I really need help! There ³ _____ (be) snakes everywhere, I'm sure!

The treatment ⁴ _____ (start) on Friday and it ⁵ _____ (be) really difficult. In the first session we ⁶ _____ (go) to the zoo to look at snakes. Ugh! Then the week after the doctor ⁷ _____ (take) a snake out of its tank and we ⁹ _____ (take) it in turns to hold it. I think I ¹⁰ _____ (wear) gloves that day!

5 ★★★ Answer the questions with *will, going to* or the present continuous.

  1 What arrangements have you got this week?

  2 What aren't you planning to do in the near future?

  3 What do you think the weather will be like next weekend?

(E)xplore prepositional phrases

6 ★★ (Circle) the correct options.

  1 My mum's terrified **in /(of)** birds so we can't have one as a pet.

  2 Dean says he's very embarrassed **of / about** the photos on his Facebook post.

  3 I can't think **in / of** anything to write about for my blog.

  4 Clara say she's got a phobia but she doesn't want to share it **about / with** us.

  5 Don't worry **about / with** taking the lift. It'll be fine.

Listening and vocabulary

Listening

1 ★ 🔊 **06** **Listen to Jordan talking about a course he's attending. What is the course about? Does he feel positive or negative about it?**

2 ★★ 🔊 **06** **Listen again. Are these sentences true (*T*) or false (*F*)?**

1 Jordan's phobia started after a visit to the country. _F_
2 He finally decided to do something after a terrifying weekend. ___
3 The course was at a hospital. ___
4 The other people on the course were relaxed. ___
5 The course helps people lose their spider phobia in three sessions. ___
6 A therapist talked about why people get phobias. ___
7 The expert explained two facts about spiders. ___
8 There are many dangerous spiders in Britain. ___
9 Jordan is the only person who is going to have hypnotherapy. ___
10 Jordan is thinking about bringing a pet spider home. ___

-ed and *-ing* adjective endings

3 ★ **Match the pairs of adjectives with the pictures.**

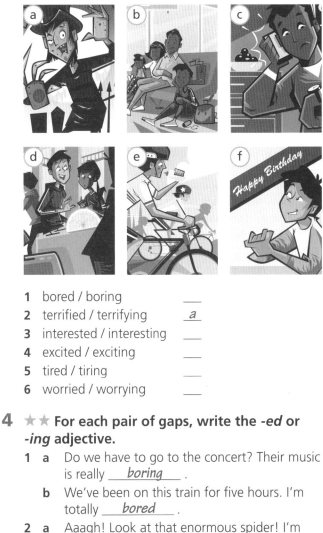

1 bored / boring ___
2 terrified / terrifying _a_
3 interested / interesting ___
4 excited / exciting ___
5 tired / tiring ___
6 worried / worrying ___

4 ★★ **For each pair of gaps, write the *-ed* or *-ing* adjective.**

1 a Do we have to go to the concert? Their music is really __boring__ .
  b We've been on this train for five hours. I'm totally __bored__ .
2 a Aaagh! Look at that enormous spider! I'm _____ of spiders.
  b The rollercoaster was _____ . I'm never going on it again.
3 a You went to bed very late last night. Aren't you _____ ?
  b We've got a new athletics coach. Her training sessions are really _____ .
4 a I've never been to a big football match before. I'm so _____ !
  b The kayaking trip was very _____ .
5 a I think climate change is _____ .
  b What a difficult exam. I'm _____ that I've failed it.
6 a This article about phobias is very _____ .
  b I've got a DVD about insects out of the library. Are you _____ ?

Language focus 2

Quantifiers

1 ★ **Complete the rules in the table. Write** *all*, *plural*, *countable* **or** *uncountable*.

1	We use *too much*, *not much* and *how much* with _____ nouns.
2	We use *too many*, *not many* and *how many* with _____ nouns.
3	We use *a lot of*, *some*, *any*, *enough*, *not enough* and *not any* with _____ nouns.

2 ★ **Complete the sentences with the words in the box.**

> ~~how many~~   not many   any (x2)
> some   too many   enough
> too much   much   how much

1 ___How many___ dangerous snakes are there in the world?
2 I've studied for 10 hours this week but I still haven't done _____ work. I'm going to fail!
3 Are there _____ clowns at this circus? Yes? Then I don't want to go.
4 _____ money have you got? I need to buy this book for school.
5 A lot of people are afraid of spiders but _____ people have got a phobia of mirrors. It's very unusual.
6 Maybe teenagers spend _____ time on their games consoles.
7 _____ people get very anxious if they can't use their mobile. It's called nomophobia!
8 Holly isn't going to come for a walk. She says there are _____ snakes round here.
9 There aren't _____ insects outside now. In the winter they all die.
10 I haven't got _____ time, but I've got enough to watch the end of this programme.

a little / a few

3 ★ **Circle the correct words in the table.**

1	Use *a few* and *a little* to talk about **small / large** quantities and amounts.
2	Use *a few / a little* with plural countable nouns.
3	Use *a few / a little* with uncountable nouns.

4 ★★ **Complete the text with *a few* or *a little*.**

Why do we love horror films? **1** ___A few___ people never watch them, but most people like being terrified! We think that **2** _____ horror is fun, not scary. A good horror film has got **3** _____ essential ingredients. You need **4** _____ horrible surprises, a lot of scary music, **5** _____ blood (not too much!), and of course, **6** _____ monsters, aliens or zombies. You don't need much money, just mix all these together, and you've got a good film!

5 ★★★ **What are the essential ingredients of … ? Choose one of the things in the box. Write four or five ideas, using quantifiers. Include at least one thing you *don't* need.**

> a computer game   a comedy programme
> a good book   a perfect birthday party

For a perfect birthday party, you don't need a lot of people, only a few good friends and some great music …

Explore opposites

6 ★★ **Complete the sentences with the opposites of the adjectives in the box.**

> lucky   ~~bad~~   sensible   unsuccessful
> dangerous   old

1 That film wasn't very ___good___ . Don't go to see it.
2 The lift isn't very _____ . It stops between floors.
3 Greg was very _____ . He won the karate competition!
4 Eddie's house is really cool. It's full of _____ furniture.
5 We went on a skiing holiday but there was no snow! We were very _____ .
6 A lot of people think that being afraid of clowns is very _____ . But it's a real phobia.

Reading

1 ★ **Read the text about Janie. What was her problem? Does she still have the problem?**

Are you EXAM-PHOBIC?

Janie was a good student. She worked hard in class, and did her homework, but she did badly in exams. Then one day her ***mind went blank***. She ***froze*** and couldn't answer any of the questions.

Most people feel a little nervous before a test. It's normal, and a few nerves can often help you do well. But for some people, like Janie, the anxiety is too strong, and it results in physical symptoms which affect their ability to think. This is called test anxiety.

Test anxiety is when you feel stressed because you have to do well. It can also happen when you sing a solo in a concert, or play an important match. In extreme cases, you ***shake***, think you are going to ***faint***, or your mind goes blank, like Janie. So what's the solution?

- **STUDY HABITS.** Many students only study for exams the night before. You can reduce test anxiety if you study more regularly. This gives you ***confidence***, and means you expect to do well.

- **POSITIVE THINKING.** Negative thoughts, like 'I know I'm going to fail this exam,' affect your confidence in yourself. Repeat positive messages to yourself.

- **LOOK AFTER YOURSELF.** Getting enough sleep and exercise, and eating healthy food before an exam can help your mind work at its best.

- *BREATHE.* Calm yourself with breathing exercises regularly, when you're *not* stressed. Do these exercises before an exam, and your body recognises them as the ***signal*** to relax.

Janie already had some good study habits, but she didn't get enough sleep. She also expected to do badly in exams. So she used these ***tips*** to help herself, and they worked! Now she can't believe she ever had test anxiety.

2 ★★ **Match the words in the box with the definitions. Use the words in *bold* in the text to help you.**

> (mind) go blank   signal   ~~shake~~   faint [*verb*]
> confidence   tip [*noun*]   breathe   freeze

1 small uncontrollable movements
  of the body _____*shake*_____
2 you cannot remember anything _____
3 a feeling that you can do
  something well _____
4 a small piece of advice _____
5 take air in and out of your body _____
6 lose consciousness _____
7 become immobile _____
8 gesture or action used to give
  an instruction _____

3 ★★ **Read the text again and answer the questions.**

1 Why was it surprising that Janie didn't do well
  in exams?
  Because she was a good student.
2 Why can a few nerves before an exam be a good
  thing?
  _____
3 Why can studying more regularly help?
  _____
4 Why should you get enough sleep, food and
  exercise?
  _____
5 When should you do breathing exercises?
  _____
6 How did Janie solve her problem?
  _____

4 ★★★ **Read the sentences. Do these people have test anxiety? Write Yes (*Y*) or No (*N*).**

1 'I think I'm going to faint!' _Y_
2 'I'm going to bed early to get a good
  night's sleep.' ___
3 'Oh no! I can't remember anything!' ___
4 'Before an exam, I do breathing exercises
  to relax.' ___
5 'I've worked hard for this exam. I know
  I can pass.' ___
6 'I know I'm going to fail. I know it!' ___

5 ★★★ **How do you feel about exams? Have you ever had any of the symptoms in the text? Do you think the solutions would work for you? Why?/Why not? Write your answers.**

Writing

An email to a friend

1 **Read Eve's email to her friend about her plans. What is she afraid of?**

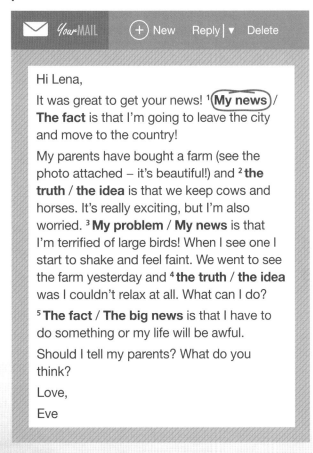

Hi Lena,

It was great to get your news! ¹(**My news**) / **The fact** is that I'm going to leave the city and move to the country!

My parents have bought a farm (see the photo attached – it's beautiful!) and ² **the truth** / **the idea** is that we keep cows and horses. It's really exciting, but I'm also worried. ³ **My problem** / **My news** is that I'm terrified of large birds! When I see one I start to shake and feel faint. We went to see the farm yesterday and ⁴ **the truth** / **the idea** was I couldn't relax at all. What can I do?

⁵ **The fact** / **The big news** is that I have to do something or my life will be awful.

Should I tell my parents? What do you think?

Love,

Eve

2 **Read the email again. Circle the correct options.**

3 **Read the email again and complete the sentences.**

1 Eve ___*doesn't live*___ in the country now.
2 She and her parents are going to live on a _____ .
3 Eve is _____ about moving.
4 She's afraid of _____ birds.
5 When she sees a bird she thinks she's going to _____ .
6 She saw the farm _____ .
7 On the farm she can't _____ .
8 She _____ told her parents about the problem.

Useful language **Introducing news and explaining things ──**

4 **Match the sentences.**

1 My big news is that I'm going to spend the summer working at a restaurant.   *b*
2 My news is that my parents are sending me to Ireland for two weeks.   ___
3 The fact is that I'm terrified of the dark.   ___
4 My news is that I'm going to do a course about social networks.   ___
5 The big news is that my family and I are going to live in Canada.   ___

a The truth is I haven't even got a Facebook account!
b The problem is that I don't know how to cook!
c And the truth is that I'm embarrassed about it.
d The problem is that I hate the winter and the snow!
e The idea is that I'll live with a family and practise my English.

Writing

5 Choose the correct options.

1 We're going to Los Angeles. I'm really (excited) / exciting.

2 We're moving to another house. It's **amazed** / **amazing**.

3 I'm afraid of the dark. I feel really **embarrassed** / **embarrassing**.

4 The truth is I hate flying and I'm really **worried** / **worrying**.

5 We live on the top floor and it's **terrified** / **terrifying**.

6 Are the sentences plans or predictions? Tick (✓) the correct box.

		plan	prediction
1	It'll be really exciting.		✓
2	We're going to live in the country.		
3	My life will be awful!		
4	It'll be a big change for me.		
5	I'm going to have my own room.		
6	My dad's going to work at a different company.		

> **WRITING TIP**
>
> Make it better! ✓ ✓ ✓
> Ask for advice at the end of your email.

7 Read the sentences. Which sentence does <u>not</u> ask for advice?

1 Should I go to a doctor about my problem?

2 I really don't know what to do.

3 What do you think I should do?

4 Do you think I should tell my mother?

5 Is it a good idea to tell someone?

8 Number the things in the list in the order they appear in the email.

what the problem is _____

an introduction _1_

a question to ask what your friend thinks _____

how you feel about the problem and why _____

some personal news _____

what you have/haven't done about the problem _____

PLAN

9 Invent a problem to write about. Make notes for each heading in Exercise 8.

WRITE

10 Write an email to a friend about your problem. Look at page 71 of the Student's Book to help you.

_____

_____

_____

_____

_____

_____

_____

_____

_____

_____

_____

_____

_____

_____

_____

_____

CHECK

11 Check your writing. Can you say YES to these questions?

• Is the information from the list in Exercise 8 in your email?

• Have you used expressions to explain the problem in your email?

• Have you used *-ed* and *-ing* adjectives correctly?

• Have you used *going to* for plans and *will* for predictions?

• Have you finished your email asking for advice?

• Are the spelling and punctuation correct?

Do you need to write a second draft?

Vocabulary
Fears

1 Complete the sentences with the words in the box. There are two extra words.

> snakes ~~flying~~ heights clowns
> insects lifts the dark birds

1 I don't like travelling by plane because I'm afraid of _flying_ .
2 I hate going to the circus because I'm afraid of _____ .
3 I usually take the stairs to the top floor because I'm afraid of _____ .
4 I don't want to go up the tower because I'm afraid of _____ .
5 Please don't switch off the lights because I'm afraid of _____ .
6 I never go to the reptile house in the zoo because I'm afraid of _____ .

Total: 5

-ed and -ing adjective endings

2 Circle the correct options.

1 She is terrified / terrifying.
2 The film is terrified / terrifying.

3 The football match is excited / exciting.
4 They are excited / exciting.

5 He is worried / worrying.
6 The results are worried / worrying.

7 She is tired / tiring.
8 The walk was tired / tiring.

Total: 7

Language focus
be going to / will / Present continuous

3 Read the conversation. Choose the correct options.

A: When **¹** are you leaving / will you leave for Japan?
B: We **²** 're leaving / 'll leave on Monday. We **³** 're flying / 'll fly direct to Tokyo. We **⁴** 're going to look round / 're looking round Tokyo for a few days and then we **⁵** 're driving / 'll drive to Kyoto for two days.
A: Sounds wonderful! You **⁶** won't be / 're not going to be bored.
B: Japan is beautiful. It **⁷** 'll be / 's being interesting to see the temples in Kyoto.
A: When **⁸** are you coming / are you going to come back?
B: On Sunday. We **⁹** won't stay / 're not staying long.

Total: 8

Quantifiers

4 Circle the correct options.

I didn't enjoy my friend's birthday party last weekend. There were too **¹** much / many people, there wasn't **²** enough / many food and there weren't **³** a little / many drinks. There weren't **⁴** any / some chairs either, so we couldn't sit down. There was too **⁵** many / much noise and I couldn't hear what people were saying. However, I ate **⁶** a lot of / a few ice cream and then I felt better. I don't go to **⁷** some / many parties because I think they're stressful!

Total: 6

a little / a few

5 Complete the sentences. Use *a little* or *a few*.

1 There are only _____ a few _____ biscuits left, so don't take them all!
2 I'm going to invite _____ friends to my party on Saturday.
3 There are _____ people in my class who are afraid of spiders.
4 It's OK to eat _____ sugar every day, but not too much!
5 My bedroom looks boring. I think I'll put _____ pictures on the wall.
6 Her sister is six, so she only gets _____ homework every day.

Total: 5

Language builder

6 Complete the conversation with the missing words. (Circle) the correct options.

> **Josh:** Let's go to the park! I **¹**___ football with some friends.
> **Justin:** Oh sorry … I **²**___ my homework yet. **³**___ your homework already?
> **Josh:** Yes, I **⁴**___ it yesterday! Why don't you join us later?
> **Justin:** I haven't played football **⁵**___ ages, I just don't have **⁶**___ time. Our teacher gives us **⁷**___ homework and then I **⁸**___ study for a test on Mondays, too.
> **Josh:** You **⁹**___ worry so much. You **¹⁰**___ to relax and have fun sometimes!
> **Justin:** Yes, but if I **¹¹**___ well this year, my parents **¹²**___ me go to summer camp!

	a	b	c
1	play	**(b)** 'm going to play	played
2	finished	've finished	haven't finished
3	You have done	Did you do	Have you done
4	finished	have finished	finish
5	on	for	since
6	many	little	enough
7	too much	too many	a lot
8	usually have to	have to usually	have usually to
9	have to	shouldn't	don't
10	have	should	must
11	don't do	won't do	will do
12	don't let	let	won't let

Total: 11

Vocabulary builder

7 (Circle) the correct options.

1 I'm not climbing up there. I'm afraid of ___ .
   a lifts   **(b)** heights   **c** high
2 I'm worried ___ the exam tomorrow.
   a of   **b** about   **c** with
3 He scored two goals in the match and he was ___ about it for a week!
   a boasting   **b** criticizing   **c** whispering
4 I'm going to try my new contact ___ today.
   a kit   **b** lessons   **c** lenses
5 I love ___ photos.
   a taking   **b** making   **c** doing
6 I'm really tired. I'm going to ___ early tonight.
   a go to the bed   **b** go to a bed   **c** go to bed
7 I didn't like the film at all. I thought it was really ___ .
   a bored   **b** boring   **c** bore
8 Jenny's idea is not silly at all. I think it's very ___ .
   a safe   **b** successful   **c** sensible
9 Can you share that video ___ your friends on Facebook?
   a about   **b** with   **c** to
10 We're going to a theme park tomorrow. I'm really ___ .
   a exciting   **b** embarrassed   **c** excited

Total: 9

Speaking

8 Complete the conversation with the words in the box.

> serious   true   joking   way
> impossible   ~~what~~   believe

> **A:** Have you heard? Sam's going to climb Mount Everest.
> **B:** ¹ _What_ ? Are you ² _____ ?
> **A:** Yes, I am. He's in a mountain climbing team.
> **B:** That's ³ _____ . Sam's afraid of heights.
> **A:** Imagine – he could be the youngest person to climb Everest.
> **B:** You're ⁴ _____ !
> **A:** No, I'm not. It's really ⁵ _____ .
> **B:** I don't ⁶ _____ you! That's incredible!
> **A:** They're leaving next week.
> **B:** No ⁷ _____ ! He didn't tell me about it.

Total: 6

Total: 57

be going to/will/Present continuous

Remember that:
- we use **be going to** to talk about future intentions
  - ✓ *I'm going to study on Saturday night.*
  - ✗ *I will study on Saturday night.*
- we use **will** to talk about predictions in the future
  - ✓ *If I can, I will call you tomorrow.*
  - ✗ *If I can, I'm going to call you tomorrow.*
- we use the present continuous to talk about future arrangements when they have a fixed date or time
  - ✓ *I'm meeting my friends at 6 o'clock.*
  - ✗ *I'm going to meet my friends at 6 o'clock.*

1 Circle the correct words.

Jim:	My dad's got a new job. My family ¹are going to move / will move to a new town.
Peter:	No way! When are you leaving?
Jim:	We ² will find / are finding out soon.
Peter:	But where ³ are you going to live / are you living ?
Jim:	I don't know! My dad ⁴ is having / will have a meeting with his boss tomorrow. He ⁵ is going to call / is calling us as soon as he knows. Then we ⁶ will decide / are deciding where to live.

Quantifiers

Remember that:
- We use **(not) many** and **a few** with plural countable nouns
  - ✓ *There were too many people on the plane.*
  - ✗ *There were too much people on the plane.*
  - ✓ *We took a few photos at the theme park.*
  - ✗ *We took a little photos at the theme park.*
- We use **(not) much** and **a little** with uncountable nouns
  - ✓ *We spent too much money at the theme park.*
  - ✗ *We spent too many money at the theme park.*
  - ✓ *We've got a little time before the bus comes.*
  - ✗ *We've got a few time before the bus comes.*

2 Circle the correct words.
1 How **much** / many time do you spend on homework?
2 Did you take **much / many** photos on holiday?
3 We had **a little / a few** money left, so we bought ice creams.
4 There wasn't **much / many** food at the party.
5 There were too **much / many** cars in the city.
6 How **much / many** people came to the match?

Prepositional phrases

Remember that:
- We use **of** after **afraid, frightened, scared, terrified**:
  - ✓ *Everybody's afraid of something.*
  - ✗ *Everybody's afraid from something.*
- We use **about** after **worried, embarrassed** and **excited**:
  - ✓ *I'm really worried about my exams.*
  - ✗ *I'm really worried for my exams.*
- We use **in** after **interested**:
  - ✓ *Everyone was interested in the article.*
  - ✗ *Everyone was interested of the article.*

3 Find and correct five more mistakes with prepositional phrases in the text.

> Everyone I know has something they are worried *about* ~~for~~! My mum is frightened for spiders. My sister Jane is scared for flying. My cousin Sally is excited about her school trip, but she's anxious of travelling. My dog, Bob, is terrified about storms! And me? I am very interested on phobias!

-ed and -ing adjectives

Remember that:
- We use adjectives ending with **-ed/-ied** to describe how people feel
  - ✓ *I am very interested in phobias.*
  - ✗ *I am very interesting in phobias.*
- We use adjectives ending with **-ing/-ying** to describe how things make us feel
  - ✓ *I think phobias are very interesting.*
  - ✗ *I think phobias are very interested.*
- Only people and animals can be *interested, excited, tired,* etc.

4 Add **-ed/ied** or **-ing/ying** to the adjectives.
1 Scarlett Johansson is frighten *ed* of spiders.
2 He's really worr _____ about his exam.
3 We had a relax _____ afternoon at the beach.
4 They're excit _____ about their trip to Brazil.
5 The roller coaster was really terrif _____ .
6 My brother thinks theme parks are bor _____ .

7 School life

Vocabulary

Life at school

1 ★ **Use the clues to complete the crossword.**

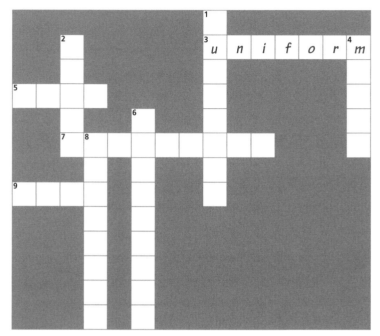

The crossword shows **3 Across** filled in as: u n i f o r m

Across

3 I hate wearing a _____ . I want to wear my own clothes to school.

5 My Science teacher gets angry if we don't _____ in our homework on time.

7 We couldn't hear the teacher because there was _____ and shouting in the classroom.

9 Our Maths teacher tells us to sit at the back of the class if we don't arrive on _____ .

Down

1 Now that Ivan is doing karate the _____ from his classmates has stopped.

2 I had to write _____ after school, so I was late home again.

4 Dad always says it's important to get good _____ at school, but my gran says it's also important to have fun!

6 I can't believe you got _____ for dropping your book on the floor!

8 Most students are really good at _____ in a test, so you never see them do it.

2 ★★ **Write the *-ing* form of words and phrases from Exercise 1.**

1 Bart Simpson does this a lot!
   *writing lines*

2 Writing things on your arm before an exam is a way to do this. _____

3 We hate this because we have to stay after school. _____

4 My school starts at 8 o'clock in the morning, so this is hard for me. _____

5 Noisy students often do this in class. _____

6 If you study hard, you'll keep on doing this. _____

3 ★★ **Complete the text. Use the correct form of the phrases from Exercise 1.**

My granddad was telling me about his school the other day. It was very strict, and if they didn't **1** _**wear a uniform**_ they had to go home and change their clothes. Students got **2**_____ for things like not sitting properly in class. He said he often had to **3**_____ , usually 'I must not talk in class'. There were physical punishments, too, if you didn't arrive **4**_____ for school, or **5**_____ in an exam. Even if a teacher heard you **6**_____ , you had to go and see the principal. He also said there was a lot of **7**_____ , but no-one told the teachers. What about rewards? I asked. He said the students who always handed in **8**_____ the next day and got **9**_____ in their exams sometimes got a boring book at the end of the year. His school was very different from ours!

4 ★★★ **How similar is your school to the school in Exercise 3? Which rewards and punishments do you think are the most effective? Write at least five sentences.**

Language focus 1

Second conditional

1 ★ **Match the sentence halves.**

1 If I got detention,   *d*
2 He wouldn't get good marks   ___
3 If students had to write lines at my school, ___
4 They wouldn't get detention   ___
5 If you went to school in England,   ___

a if they did their homework.
b you'd have to wear a uniform.
c if he didn't cheat in tests.
d I wouldn't be able to go to my piano lesson.
e they'd probably behave better.

2 ★★ **Complete the sentences about a school in Singapore. Use the correct form of the verbs in brackets.**

1 If you __went__ (go) to this school,
  you _'d start_ (start) at 7.35 in the morning.
2 All the lessons _____ (be) in English
  if you _____ (study) there.
3 You _____ (not be) allowed to wear
  earrings if you _____ (be) a boy.
4 If a girl_____ (break) the rules, she
  _____ (get) detention.
5 If a boy or a girl _____ (not wear)
  their uniform, the school _____
  (send) them home.
6 If a student _____ (not get) good
  marks, he or she _____ (go) to an
  after-school homework club.

3 ★★ **Complete the conversation with the second conditional. Use the verbs in the box.**

| ~~be~~ give ask not spend |
| help improve live go |

A: Oh dear, I failed the Maths exam! I hate
Maths! If I **1**_____ _were_ _____ better at it,
I **2**_____ hours every week on my
homework. It's frustrating!
B: What about your teacher? She
3_____ you if you **4**_____
her, I'm sure.
A: Maybe but she's very strict. My mum wants
me to have a Maths tutor. She thinks if a
tutor **5**_____ me extra lessons, it
6_____ my marks.
B: She's probably right. Do you know, if
we **7**_____ in Singapore, we
8_____ to an after-school homework
club every night? Most teenagers there do.
A: Every night? How awful!

4 ★★★ **Complete the sentences with your own ideas.**

1 It would be amazing if… _I got the best mark_
          in the class for my test.
2 I wouldn't wear a uniform if… _____
  _____
3 I wouldn't complain if… _____
  _____
4 I would be worried if… _____
  _____
5 I would cheat in a test if… _____
  _____
6 I would have more time to do what I wanted if…
  _____

5 ★★★ **Imagine you were the head teacher at your school. What would you change? Write at least five sentences.**

Listening and vocabulary

Listening

1 ★ 🔊 **07** **Listen to Kesia talking to her dad about her education. What does she want to do? Does her dad agree?**

2 ★★ 🔊 **07** **Read the sentences. Listen again and circle the correct options.**
1 Kesia is **14** / **16** years old.
2 She says she **never has fun** / **doesn't like the rules** at school.
3 She thinks she'd learn **more** / **less** if she didn't go to school.
4 She found out about home education from **the Internet** / **her friends**.
5 Her dad thinks home education would be **easy** / **difficult** to organise.
6 With home education you **can** / **can't** study outside the classroom.
7 Kesia **would** / **wouldn't** be able to see her friends if she's not at school.
8 Kesia **often** / **never** does homework with her friends.
9 Kesia's dad decides **he will talk to her mother** / **she should leave school now** .
10 Kesia needs to find out more about **home education** / **university** .

make and do

3 ★ **Complete the phrases with make or do.**
1 ___make___ friends
2 _____ your homework
3 _____ something interesting
4 _____ a phone call
5 _____ a mess
6 _____ decisions
7 _____ the right thing
8 _____ a mistake
9 _____ an exercise
10 _____ a noise

4 ★★ **Complete the sentences with the phrases in Exercise 3.**
1 You have to _do your homework_ or you can't go to the party.
2 I hate shopping with Liam. It's impossible for him to _____ about what to buy.
3 Can you wait for a minute? I just need to _____ to a friend.
4 It's really easy for Sue to _____ . She knows everyone!
5 I did the wrong homework! I always _____ when I copy from the board!
6 Do you think I should buy Annie a present to say thank you for helping me? I want to _____ .
7 Look at the kitchen! Why do you always _____ when you cook?
8 Let's _____ this weekend, like watching horror films at your house.

Language focus 2

Second conditional questions

1 ★★ **Put the words in the correct order to make questions.**

1 at / you / they / prize / you / school, / If / what / won / a / give / would / ?
If you won a prize at school, what would they give you?

2 you / if / your / detention / tell / you / got / parents / Would / ?
_____
_____

3 If / you / be / rule, / change / would / school / one / could / it / what / ?
_____
_____

4 you / another / friends / Would / went / if / make / quickly / to / you / school?
_____
_____

5 you / decision, / make / an / talk / wanted / to / If / important / you / who / would / to / ?
_____
_____

6 would / your / fun / do / If / friends / something / tonight, / what / did / they / ?
_____
_____

2 ★ **Match the answers with the questions in Exercise 1.**

a We'd start class at 11 o'clock, not 8 o'clock!
b They'd probably go skateboarding.
c No, I wouldn't.
d They'd give me a book and a certificate.
e Yes, I would. I'm quite sociable.
f I would probably talk to my sister.

1 _d_
2 ___
3 ___
4 ___
5 ___
6 ___

3 ★★ **Complete the conversation. Use the correct form of the verbs in brackets or a short answer.**

A: What kind of teacher ¹___would you be___ (you be)?
B: What do you mean?
A: Well, if ²_____ (you be) a teacher, ³_____ (you be) strict?
B: No, I ⁴_____ – definitely not! I prefer teachers who don't punish you.
A: Well, I'm not sure. What ⁵_____ (you do) if ⁶_____ (the students not listen to you)?
B: I don't know. ⁷_____ (you give) detention?
A: Probably. ⁸_____ (the students respect) you less if ⁹_____ (you not give) them detention?
B: Maybe, yes. But really, ¹⁰_____ (you want) to be a teacher?
A: Yes, ¹¹_____ . I think I'd enjoy it.
B: Oh! What ¹²_____ (you teach) then?
A: Physics, probably.

4 ★★★ **Imagine you are home educated. Write the questions. Then answer them for you.**

> what / study?   do exams?   where / go?
> what / be the best thing about it?
> miss anything at school?

If you were home educated, … *what would you study? I'd probably study Geography, History and …*

Explore phrasal verbs (3)

5 ★★ Circle **the correct options.**

1 I wrote **off** / (**out**) all the names carefully before I made a decision.
2 Would you like to try **out** / **on** our new computer software?
3 Small children pick **out** / **up** a lot of new words from their parents.
4 I spent hours thinking about it but I couldn't work **out** / **off** the answer.
5 The teacher found **out** / **off** they were cheating because they had the same answers.

Reading

1 ★ **Read Ted's text about an experiment at his school. What is a 'secret student'? Did it work at Ted's school?**

You might be the 'SECRET STUDENT' today!

Last year my school tried a new way to get students to *behave* better in class. It's called the 'secret student', and the idea is not to punish bad behaviour but reward good behaviour *instead*. If your class gets enough points, they get a prize at the end of the year.

Here's what happens. Every morning the class teacher chooses a secret student *at random* – by picking a name from a box. This person represents the class all day. In every lesson the teacher monitors him or her, and gives a tick for good behaviour or a cross for bad behaviour. At the end of the day, the *class* is awarded a point if the secret student has got more ticks than crosses. The *crucial* thing about this system is that if you were the secret student you wouldn't know, so everyone has to behave well to make sure the class gets a point. The teachers only *reveal* the identity of that day's secret student if they award a point, but if the student doesn't get a point their identity stays secret.

The idea of the secret student is to make everyone feel their behaviour has consequences for the whole class, not just for them individually. It also means students *encourage* each other to behave: 'You could be the secret student, stop talking!' The teachers also *warn* students who start behaving badly: 'Jan, you might be the secret student! Do you want a tick? Then sit down!' In the end everybody becomes more responsible, and it brings the class together.

It certainly worked in my class. Our behaviour was much better and we got 108 points, which was enough for a day at a theme park after our exams. We had an amazing time, so it was definitely *worth it*!

Secret Student
Tuesday 25 April

Henry Clyde

Class	Behaviour
1	✓
2	✗
3	✓
4	✓
5	✓
6	✗

2 ★ ★ **Complete the sentences with the words in *bold* from the text.**

1 My parents always __encourage__ me to try lots of different activities.
2 I must _____ you. If I see anyone cheating, they will get a zero!
3 If you can't come tomorrow, you can come on Thursday _____ .
4 I had to train really hard all winter but it was _____ . I won a silver medal!
5 They choose the numbers in the Christmas lottery _____ .
6 Next week they will _____ the winners of the short story competition.
7 Polly, stop hitting Peter! If you don't _____ , you won't go to the circus.
8 The expert said that lots of practice is _____ if you want to get better.

3 ★ ★ **Read the text again. Are these sentences true (*T*) or false (*F*)? Correct the false sentences.**

1 Ted's school has used this method for five years. *F*
   They started it last year.
2 The method rewards students for good behaviour.
   _____
3 One student represents all the students in the class.
   _____
4 Each lesson has a different secret student.
   _____
5 The teachers give points for every lesson.
   _____
6 Only one person knows who the secret student is.
   _____
7 The students try to make sure everyone behaves.
   _____
8 If you get enough points, you can do something fun.
   _____

4 ★ ★ ★ **What do you think of the 'secret student' idea? Do you think it would work with your class? What would happen? Write your ideas.**

Writing

A problem page

1 **Read the advice leaflet. Who is it for?**

HOW TO MAKE FRIENDS
AT A NEW SCHOOL!

It's hard to change schools and leave all your friends. The problem is that in a new school everything is different. You even get lost going to your classroom! So if you're at a new school, how can you make friends fast?

- The most important thing is you **¹ can / must** be yourself – don't try to change your personality to suit other people. When people discover your personality, they will accept you.

- **² Think carefully / Make sure** about making a good impression. You **³ never / should** dress in clothes you feel comfortable in but nothing too extreme!

- **⁴ Never / Make sure** sit alone at the back of the class. Always try to sit with other people in class or in the canteen.

- You might be nervous, but **⁵ don't / make sure** you're nice to people, and **⁶ don't / think carefully** be rude. Keep smiling and try to look interested.

- If you see someone else on their own, you **⁷ don't / should** go and talk to them. They might be new at the school too and need a friend!

- You **⁸ could also / also could** try to get involved with activities and join after-school clubs. You might find people who are interested in doing the same things as you.

Stay positive and you'll soon make friends!

2 **Read the advice leaflet again. Circle the correct options.**

3 **Read the leaflet again. Match the questions with the answers.**

1 What's the problem with starting a new school?	_d_	**a** A positive one.
2 Why shouldn't you change your personality?	___	**b** They are also alone.
3 Where shouldn't you sit?	___	**c** Join activities and go to after-school clubs.
4 How should you behave?	___	**d** Everything is new.
5 What kind of attitude is best?	___	**e** Smile and be nice.
6 What's the best way to look?	___	**f** People will accept the way you are.
7 How can you recognise another new student?	___	**g** On your own at the back of the class.
8 How can you meet people with the same interests?	___	**h** Like you are interested.

Writing

Useful language Summarising a problem and giving advice

4 Complete the sentences with the words in the box.

tell ~~also~~ really say could possible

1 The problem is not only that you feel stress but _____*also*_____ that it affects your health.
2 It's _____ that you're trying to do too much.
3 I think you should _____ the truth.
4 You _____ that you can't relax but you have to.
5 You _____ also tell your teacher.
6 I _____ hope this helps.

5 Match the sentence halves.

1 If you are feeling stressed,   *c*
2 If you're not sleeping well,   ___
3 If you can't study,   ___
4 If you've got exams,   ___
5 If there's bullying in your school,   ___

a keep trying to do a bit every day.
b tell your teacher or the principal.
c take deep breaths and relax.
d do more exercise – but not before you go to bed!
e don't leave your studying to the last minute.

> **WRITING TIP**
>
> Make it better! ✓ ✓ ✓
> We always use the *-ing* form of a verb after a preposition.

6 Choose the correct options.

1 It's hard (to concentrate) / concentrating sometimes.
2 Keep on **to try** / **trying** even if you fail.
3 Think about **to change** / **changing** your diet.
4 If you're not interested in **to do** / **doing** an activity, don't do it!
5 Try to **keep** / **keeping** your bedroom tidy.

> **WRITING TIP**
>
> Make it better! ✓ ✓ ✓
> End the leaflet with something positive.

7 Read the sentences. Which one is <u>not</u> positive?

1 Stay happy and don't give up.
2 Don't forget: you can do it!
3 Believe in yourself and you'll do it!
4 Remember these rules.

8 Number the things in the list in the order they appear in the advice leaflet.

a final sentence to make people feel positive   ___
who the leaflet is for, and a question for them   ___
a title   *1*
several tips (pieces of advice)   ___
an explanation of the problem   ___

PLAN

9 You are going to write an advice leaflet about how to avoid stress at school. Make notes about the things in Exercise 8.

WRITE

10 Write your advice leaflet. Look at page 83 of the Student's Book to help you.

_____
_____
_____
_____
_____
_____
_____
_____
_____
_____
_____
_____
_____
_____
_____
_____
_____

CHECK

11 Check your writing. Can you say YES to these questions?

- Is the information in Exercise 8 in your leaflet?
- Have you introduced the advice with different expressions?
- Have you used conditionals in your writing?
- Are the *-ing* verbs and infinitives correct?
- Does the leaflet end with a positive message?
- Are the spelling and punctuation correct?

Do you need to write a second draft?

Vocabulary
Life at school

1 Complete the sentences with the words in box.

| detention   bullying   marks   cheating |
| uniform   time   shout   lines |

1 We can wear jeans and T-shirts to school –
we don't have to wear a ___uniform___ .

2 Dave didn't do his homework and so he got
_____ .

3 Students get good _____ if they show
they've worked hard.

4 You can't copy from another student – that's
_____ .

5 You mustn't _____ at your classmates –
it's very rude.

6 Sometimes we have to write _____
when we behave badly.

7 Cindy is always late for class. She has problems
being on _____ .

8 You shouldn't be aggressive with students that
are younger than you – that's _____ .

Total: 7

make and *do*

2 Complete the table with the words in the box.

| homework   a decision   phone calls |
| something fun   ~~friends~~   a mistake |
| the right thing   a mess   an exercise   a noise |

Make	Do
friends	

Total: 9

Language focus
Second conditional

3 (Circle) the correct options.

1 If you **would study /(studied)** harder, you
(would get)/ got better marks in your tests.

2 He **wouldn't get / didn't get** so many detentions,
if he **would be / was** on time.

3 If the teacher **would see / saw** you cheating, she
wouldn't give / didn't give you good marks.

4 We **would have / had** more free time if we
wouldn't have / didn't have so much homework.

5 If I **would be / was** a bit taller, I **would be / was**
on the school netball team.

6 She **would be / was** lonely if she **wouldn't go /
didn't go** to school.

Total: 5

Second conditional questions

4 Complete the second conditional questions.
Use *you* and the correct form of the verbs in
brackets.

1 What ___would you say___ (say) if
___you met___ (meet) your favourite musician?

2 If _____ (have) a car, where
_____ (go)?

3 What _____ (do) if
_____ (not have to) go to school?

4 If _____ (win) the lottery,
_____ (spend) all the money
immediately?

5 _____ (fly) to the Moon if
_____ (have) enough money?

6 If _____ (not pass) an exam, what
_____ (say) to your parents?

Total: 5

Language builder

5 Complete the conversation with the missing words. (Circle) the correct options.

Sally: ¹___ on time for school?
Julie: Yes. I ²___ late this term yet!
Sally: I've been late three times ³___ , and I ⁴___ detention last week.
Julie: That's not good. ⁵___ play in the school football team this year?
Sally: I probably ⁶___ because I've got ⁷___ work to do. I ⁸___ the team if I ⁹___ exams at the end of this year. How about you?
Julie: I ¹⁰___ yet. I ¹¹___ join the tennis team. The problem is there aren't many tennis courts at school.
Sally: If you ¹²___ to school early, you'd get a place on a court easily!

1	ⓐ	Are you usually	**b**	Are usually you	**c**	Do you usually
2	**a**	was	**b**	have been	**c**	haven't been
3	**a**	still	**b**	yet	**c**	already
4	**a**	was getting	**b**	've got	**c**	got
5	**a**	You are going	**b**	Are you going to	**c**	Are you
6	**a**	won't	**b**	will	**c**	might
7	**a**	too many	**b**	too much	**c**	a little
8	**a**	joined	**b**	'll join	**c**	'd join
9	**a**	hadn't	**b**	didn't have	**c**	wouldn't have
10	**a**	've decided	**b**	don't decide	**c**	haven't decided
11	**a**	might	**b**	'll	**c**	'm
12	**a**	came	**b**	come	**c**	were coming

Total: 11

Vocabulary builder

6 (Circle) the correct options.
1 You've ___ a real mess of your homework. Do it again!
 a done **ⓑ** made **c** had
2 The school rules are clear. You must be ___ time every day.
 a at **b** of **c** on
3 Vicki doesn't seem very worried ___ getting detention.
 a of **b** about **c** with
4 If you ___ a cold, you'll miss the big match on Saturday.
 a catch **b** take **c** make
5 If I had more time, I'd ___ with my friends more.
 a keep on **b** set up **c** hang out
6 You should ___ the right thing and tell the teacher.
 a do **b** make **c** have
7 Please ___ your homework on Monday.
 a go up **b** try out **c** hand in
8 She can't sleep. She's afraid of ___ .
 a the dark **b** dark **c** a dark
9 It's ___ today. I'm so cold!
 a freezing **b** heat wave **c** snowstorm
10 At the market there was a ___ throwing ten balls in the air!
 a busker **b** juggler **c** mural

Total: 9

Speaking

7 Put the sentences in the correct order to make a conversation asking for and giving advice.

___ **Julie:** Have you tried talking to your parents?

___ **Julie:** Oh dear. If I were you, I'd talk to the teacher about it.

___ **Julie:** What's the problem?

_1_ **Zoe:** Hi Julie! I need your advice.

___ **Zoe:** I can't finish all my homework. What do you think I should do?

___ **Zoe:** I can't do that. She'll think I'm lazy!

___ **Zoe:** Yes, maybe that's the best idea.

Total: 6

Total: 52

Second conditional

Remember that:
- we use *if + subject + the past simple* in the action/situation clause
  - ✓ *If I knew the answer, I would tell you.*
- we use *would/wouldn't + infinitive* to talk about the consequences of the action/situation.
  - ✓ *If I knew the answer, I would tell you.*
- We don't use *will* to talk about the consequences of the action/situation
  - ✗ *If I knew the answer, I ~~will~~ tell you.*
- We don't use *would/wouldn't + infinitive* in the same clause as *if*.
  - ✗ *If I ~~would know~~, I would tell you.*

1 **Are the sentences correct? Correct the incorrect sentences.**
1. If I would go to England, I would visit Cambridge.
   If I went to England, I would visit Cambridge.
2. They will be very happy if they went to a Free School.
3. If I had the choice, I would go on holiday.
4. I won't go to bed early if it would be the holidays.

Second conditional questions

Remember that:
We form questions about the results of imaginary situations using *would(n't) + subject + verb*. The subject comes between *would(n't)* and the main verb.
- ✓ *What would you do if you saw someone cheating?*
- ✗ *What ~~you would~~ do if you saw someone cheating?*
- ✓ *If you saw someone cheating, what would you do?*
- ✗ *If you saw someone cheating, what ~~you would~~ do?*

2 **Complete the second conditional questions with *would* and the words in brackets.**
1. *What would your parents do* (do / your parents / what) if you were unhappy at school?
2. _____ (go / they) to a Free School if they had the choice?
3. If you could live anywhere, _____ (live / you / where)?
4. _____ buy / you / what) if you had a million pounds?

want, choose and *decide*

Remember that:
We use the **infinitive** with *to* after *want, choose,* and *decide*
- ✓ *I don't want to do the exam tomorrow.*
- ✗ *I don't want ~~do~~ the exam tomorrow.*
- ✗ *I don't want ~~doing~~ the exam tomorrow.*

3 **Find and correct seven more mistakes with *want, choose* and *decide* in the text.**

Everyone wants ~~doing~~ to do different things on Saturday. I don't know what to do!
Sarah wants go to the cinema, but Amy wants to go shopping. If I choose spending the day with Amy, Sarah will be upset. My mum and dad want visit my grandparents, but if my brother decides staying at home, I want to stay at home, too! If I tell my parents I don't want visit my grandparents, they'll be angry. If I could choose doing anything, I would play videogames with Mark, but he can't decide what do either!

make and *do*

Remember that:
- We use *do* with nouns for activities
  - ✓ *We often do a quiz in class.*
  - ✗ *We often ~~make a quiz~~ in class.*
  - ✓ *I usually do my homework on Sunday.*
  - ✗ *I usually ~~make my homework~~ on Sunday.*
- We use *make* with nouns when we create or produce something new
  - ✓ *I made a lot of mistakes in the exam.*
  - ✗ *I ~~did a lot of mistakes~~ in the exam.*
  - ✓ *You should make a list of your ideas.*
  - ✗ *You should ~~do a list~~ of your ideas.*

4 **Complete the sentences with the correct form of *do* or *make*.**
1. She's ___made___ a lot of new friends at school.
2. I couldn't hear because my brother was _____ too much noise.
3. You would sleep better if you _____ more exercise.
4. Did you _____ anything interesting at the weekend?
5. You've _____ such a mess in your room!
6. Do you like _____ sports at your school?

8 Green planet

Vocabulary

Materials

1 ⭐ **Find ten words for materials in the wordsquare.**

p	m	e	t	a	l	g	b	o	s	a	p
r	e	t	h	v	m	a	r	o	h	p	l
o	t	l	e	a	t	h	e	r	a	z	a
c	b	q	u	a	l	b	z	p	v	o	s
e	l	r	c	a	r	h	e	m	p	w	t
m	e	m	i	t	o	r	n	r	o	l	i
e	g	g	r	c	c	r	k	o	c	e	c
n	u	l	b	i	k	u	d	n	o	a	y
t	y	a	a	p	l	s	o	f	t	n	e
a	w	f	u	s	w	i	s	a	t	e	l
l	a	c	k	i	s	t	r	e	o	b	l
k	r	u	b	b	e	r	q	a	n	d	o

2 ⭐ **Complete the sentences. Use the first letter to help you.**

1 Put on those yellow r _ubber gloves_ if you're going to wash the dishes.
2 This table is made of w_____ from a sustainable forest.
3 He's allergic to artificial fibres, so he usually wears clothes made from pure organic c_____ .
4 Vegans don't eat or use animal products, so they don't wear l_____ jackets or shoes.
5 The ancient Egyptians wrote on papyrus but the Chinese invented p_____ in about 200 BC.
6 Gold is not the most expensive m_____ in the world. Platinum and rhodium cost more.
7 The ancient Romans used b_____ and c_____ for many of their buildings.
8 In a lot of discos people drink out of p_____ glasses, because g_____ ones could break.

3 ★★ **Match the materials in Exercise 1 with the objects.**

1 houses, fireplaces, walls   _bricks_
2 sofas, belts, shoes   _____
3 floors, stairs, plant pots   _____
4 saxophones, spoons, cans   _____
5 toys, pens, bottles   _____
6 windows, mirrors, bottles   _____
7 notebooks, cards, boxes   _____
8 car tyres, children's balls, kitchen gloves   _____
9 pencils, cupboards, tables   _____
10 T-shirts, jeans, rugs   _____

4 ★★ **Complete the text about Sue's living room.**

This picture is our new living room. Mum and Dad have made big changes! The floor is [1] _wood_ with lots of rugs, and one wall and the fireplace are now the original [2]_____ . The other walls have got [3]_____ with tree designs painted by hand. The old sofa has gone and now we've got a fantastic [4]_____ one. The windows have got beautiful green [5]_____ curtains. The new dining table is very modern. It's got a [6]_____ top with [7]_____ legs. Honestly, it could be out of a magazine! The only horrible thing is that cheap [8]_____ model of a spaceship I made when I was six. My mum loves it and keeps it on the TV!

5 ★★★ **Find objects in your bedroom for the materials. Write the names of the objects and the materials. Use a dictionary if necessary. Can you find all ten materials?**

Object name   Material(s)
photo frame   _metal, glass and plastic_

Language focus 1

Present simple passive

1 ★ **Match the sentence halves.**

1 The metal rhodium is ___f___
2 Old tyres are ___
3 Plastic bags are ___
4 Modern bricks are ___
5 New houses are ___
6 Car windows are ___
7 Small amounts of gold are ___

a made from plastic and glass.
b recycled for artificial football pitches.
c built to be more energy-efficient.
d found in the stomachs of whales.
e used to make mobile phones.
f found in South Africa.
g heated to high temperatures before use in buildings.

2 ★★ **Write passive sentences with the prompts.**

1 Most glass / produce / in big factories
Most glass is produced in big factories.

2 Glass / make / with sand and other minerals
_____

3 They / melt together / at 1700 °C
_____

4 Other materials / add / to produce different colours
_____

5 Glass / use / in many important industries
_____

6 Before glass / recycle / it / separate / into different colours
_____

7 When glass / recycle / no material / lose
_____

3 ★★ **Complete the text with the active or passive form of the verbs in brackets.**

Because most people ¹___replace___ (replace) their mobile phone every two years or less, about 125 million phones ²_____ (throw) in the bin every year in the USA. The problem is that many mobiles ³_____ (contain) dangerous metals, like lead, mercury and cadmium, so if they ⁴_____ (throw) away they ⁵_____ (pollute) the environment. Now, organisations like 'Call2Recycle' ⁶_____ (offer) to take your old phone for recycling. Your old phone ⁷_____ (collect), and then it ⁸_____ (sell) back to the company that made it. Then either it ⁹_____ (sell) again in another country, or it ¹⁰_____ (take) to pieces for the materials, like plastic, glass and metal, and the electronic components.

4 ★★★ **Answer the questions. Use the present simple passive.**

1 What material are the shoes you are wearing today made of?
_____

2 What happens to your old mobile phones?
_____

3 What does your town do about recycling?
_____

4 What happens at your school to help the environment?
_____

5 What happens at home?
_____

5 ★★★ **Think about your town or city. What happens there every day? Write sentences. Use the present simple passive.**

1 *The rubbish is collected from the streets.*
2 _____
3 _____
4 _____
5 _____
6 _____

Listening and vocabulary

Listening

1 ★★ 🔊 **08** **Listen to a radio programme called 'Everyday problems'. What can you do with your old gadgets? What should you never do?**

You can _____

or _____ .

You should never _____ .

2 ★★ 🔊 **08** **Listen again and complete the sentences.**

1 Most homes have got things they don't want, like _*games consoles*_ , _____ , _____ and tablets.

2 Often it's because we buy new, _____ , _____ versions.

3 Monica says there are _____ categories, things _____ and things _____ .

4 For the first category, the options are: _____ online or _____ to charity.

5 Some _____ and _____ look for old gadgets for students.

6 When charities are given old gadgets, they are _____ and _____ , or _____ .

7 Electronics can contain metals like _____ and _____ .

8 There are lots of companies that _____ .

9 You shouldn't throw gadgets in the rubbish because they can _____ .

10 The information about useful organisations is _____ the programme's _____ .

Energy issues

3 ★★ ⟨Circle⟩ **the correct options.**

1 My dad says we need to **turn down** /⟨**reduce**⟩ the gas we use.

2 If you want to pay less, you have to **consume** / **save** less electricity.

3 We're trying to **consume** / **save** money by **turning down** / **switching off** the water temperature in the shower.

4 Who **wastes** / **leaves on standby** the most electricity in your house?

5 My sister never **wastes** / **switches off** her computer! She often leaves it on all night.

6 When you **leave** / **reduce** the TV on standby, it's still consuming energy.

4 ★★ **Complete the advice with words from Exercise 3.**

Easy ways to go GREEN!

- Always ¹ _*switch off*_ the lights when you leave a room or before you go out.

- Don't leave your electronic devices on ² _____ when you go to sleep. All those little red or green lights ³ _____ more energy than you think!

- Don't ⁴ _____ water. Have shorter showers, and when you brush your teeth don't use water until the end.

- ⁵ _____ how much meat you eat by going vegetarian one day a week.

- ⁶ _____ the heating and put on a jumper.

- ⁷ _____ plastic bags and bottles so you can use them again.

Language focus 2

Past simple passive

1 ★ **Complete the sentences with the past simple passive. Add *by* where necessary.**

1 In Ancient China windows _____were made of_____ paper because they didn't have glass. (make)

2 Cave paintings show that leather clothing _____ people who lived 12,000 years ago. (wear)

3 The World Wide Web _____ until the 1990s. (not develop)

4 The first rubber boots _____ in France in 1853. (produce)

5 The potato came to Europe from Peru. It _____ Spanish sailors. (bring)

6 The first lightbulb _____ Edison, but he got the money. (not invent)

7 The first rules of football _____ (write down) in Cambridge in 1848.

Past simple passive questions

2 ★★ **Write past simple passive questions about these important discoveries. Then match the questions with the answers.**

1 When / X-rays / discover?
When were X-rays discovered? _____c_____

2 Who / penicillin / discover / by / 1928?
_____ ___

3 What / discover / Alfred Nobel / 1866?
_____ ___

4 What / develop / Michael Faraday / 1821?
_____ ___

5 When / the magnifying glass / develop?
_____ ___

6 Who / the first motor car / make / by?
_____ ___

7 What / make / in the 1920s / by John Logie Baird?
_____ ___

a Dynamite.
b Karl Benz, in 1886.
c In 1895, by Wilhelm Röntgen.
d In 1250, by Roger Bacon.
e The television.
f Doctor Alexander Fleming.
g The electric motor.

3 ★★★ **Complete the text with the past simple form of the verbs in brackets.**

Q: Who [1] _____was_____ Greenpeace _____set up_____ (set up) by?

A: No-one's really sure! Lots of people contributed.

Q: When and where [2] _____ Greenpeace _____ (start)?

A: In Canada in 1971, but it [3] _____ (not call) Greenpeace at first. A group of activists went to protest against an underground nuclear explosion in Alaska. Their boat [4] _____ (stop) and the nuclear test [5] _____ (not prevent), but, because of the campaign, a few months later all nuclear activity at the island [6] _____ (end) by the US government. That was the beginning of Greenpeace.

Q: When [7] _____ Greenpeace International _____ (create)?

A: In 1979. Several Greenpeace groups in different countries [8] _____ (combine) to make one worldwide organisation. Later an office [9] _____ (open) in Amsterdam, and soon Greenpeace activists [10] _____ (find) campaigning all over the world!

4 ★★★ **What five discoveries and inventions do you think were most important for the way we live now? Write past passive sentences. Use the Internet!**

An electric current was produced by Alessandro Volta in 1800.

Explore phrasal verbs (4)

5 ★★ **Complete the sentences with the correct form of the verbs in the box.**

> bring down   keep on   put up
> ~~cut down~~   knock down

1 A lot of trees _____were cut down_____ to make way for the new road.

2 I couldn't do it the first time, but I _____ trying and I learned.

3 They _____ a lot of houses in this street since we moved here.

4 If we plant trees around our house, it _____ the temperature.

5 Our old school _____ last year to build a completely new one.

Reading

1 ★ **Read the text about drinks cans. Choose the correct summary.**

  a How you can become a millionaire selling drinks in cans.

  b How recycling cans is better for the environment.

  c How we can help the environment by not buying drinks in cans.

WHAT 'CAN' WE DO?

475 billion cans of drink are sold in the world every year. What happens to all these empty aluminium cans? Amazingly, a lot of them are recycled! It takes 100 years for an aluminium can to **decompose** in a **landfill**. So recycling makes sense.

Aluminium doesn't **occur** naturally. It's made from bauxite in a process called smelting. Producing aluminium is **energy-intensive**. Bauxite is extracted by **mining**, which is expensive and creates environmental problems. Bauxite mining **harms** forests, which affects plants and animals, and the chemicals which are used in the process affect the health of people living there.

Recycling reduces the need to mine bauxite. Recycling aluminium consumes only 5% of the energy needed to produce it by mining and smelting. In fact, making *one* can with recycled aluminium saves enough energy to **run** a television for three hours!

Aluminium is one of the most common materials in modern life. It's the cheapest material to recycle, and can be recycled indefinitely because it isn't damaged by the process. Cans are also one of the easiest things to recycle – new drinks cans appear in the shops only six weeks after recycling!

In some countries people pay extra for each can they buy. If they recycle the can or take it back to a shop, they get this money back. Many places have got special machines where cans are **crushed**, and you get a ticket saying how many cans you recycled so you can reclaim the money. In Sweden, where this is very successful, 92% of cans are recycled. In Britain, people sell empty cans for charity. There are several hundred places that buy cans and then recycle them. Just imagine – if every can in the UK were recycled like this, it would raise over £30 million a year for good causes!

2 ★★ **Match the words in *bold* from the text with the definitions.**

  1 disintegrate   *decompose*

  2 pushed down into a small space _____

  3 exist somewhere _____

  4 has a bad effect on or damages _____

  5 a large place where rubbish is put in the ground _____

  6 extracting minerals from the ground

      _____

  7 give a machine the energy to work _____

  8 using a lot of energy _____

3 ★★ **Read the text again and answer the questions.**

  1 What happens to most drinks cans?
    They are recycled.

  2 What is aluminium made from?
    _____

  3 What two problems about mining this does the text mention?
    _____

  4 Why is recycling a better alternative to mining?
    _____

  5 What three advantages are there when recycling aluminium?
    _____

  6 How long is the whole recycling process?
    _____

  7 What happens in some countries to encourage recycling?
    _____

  8 How do we know this works well in Sweden?
    _____

  9 What happens in Britain?
    _____

  10 Why can you make a lot of money doing this?
    _____

4 ★★★ **What happens to cans in your country? Which of the ways explained in the article do you think is best? What do you think is the best way to stop people just throwing cans away? Write four or five sentences.**

Writing

A newspaper article

1 Read Luke's article for his school newspaper. Why will he be on TV?

Last month I went to a meeting about saving water. The event was organised by a local TV channel, and afterwards my family volunteered to try to reduce the amount of water we use. 'How do we save water?' ¹ _____asked_____ my dad.

The TV company suggested easy ways to save water. 'One of them is a five-minute limit on showers,' they ² _____ . Another was to stop wasting water while we brushed our teeth. 'You only really need water at the end,' they ³ _____ . Then one day they came to our house: 'We want to film you at home!' they ⁴ _____ us.

A TV crew came to our house when we started and again yesterday. The first time they didn't film me, but this time I was filmed switching on the dishwasher! It's great. My family have used these ideas and saved water, and we'll be on TV!

2 Complete Luke's article for his school newspaper. Use the words in the box.

> explained   told   ~~asked~~   said

3 Read the article again and answer the questions.

1 What was the meeting about?
   Reducing the water you use at home.

2 Who organised it?
   _____

3 What do Luke's family have to do?
   _____

4 What is the maximum time for a shower to save water?
   _____

5 When doesn't Luke need to use water?
   _____

6 How does he feel about the experience?
   _____

Useful language   Using direct speech ⎯

> **WRITING TIP** ⋯⋯⋯⋯⋯
>
> **Make it better! ✓ ✓ ✓**
> Use direct speech to show the reader exactly what someone said – it makes your writing more interesting.

4 Write these sentences in direct speech.

1 He explained that we are participating in a TV programme.
   You are participating in a TV programme.

2 He asked me how much water I use.
   _____

3 They explained that it's very easy to save water.
   _____

4 He told me it'll be on TV tomorrow.
   _____

5 They said we use too much water.
   _____

5 Circle the correct time linkers.

1 We went to a meeting and **after** / **afterwards** they told us about the programme.

2 They told us to turn off the TV **while** / **when** we went to bed.

3 **One** / **A** day, a TV crew came to my house.

4 I watched an interesting TV programme **the last week** / **last week**.

5 He'll have to do it again but **this time** / **that time** on film.

Writing

6 Complete the sentences with the active or passive form of the verbs in brackets.

1 The TV crew ___*filmed*___ (film) me switching off lights in the house.

2 The meeting _____ (organise) by a local TV channel.

3 They _____ (explain) different ways to save energy.

4 We _____ (ask) lots of questions about different habits.

5 They _____ (work out) how much energy we could save in a month.

6 All the videos _____ (post) online the week after the programme.

> **WRITING TIP**
>
> Make it better! ✓ ✓ ✓
> Give background information at the beginning of the article to explain to the reader why something happened.

7 Read the sentences. Which one does not give background information?

1 A TV channel sent us a letter asking if we'd like to participate in a TV programme.

2 My family and I will be on TV next month!

3 Last month I wrote to a TV channel about one of their programmes.

4 Last Sunday about 200 people went to the local TV station for an interview.

5 In March, my family found out we were going to be part of a TV programme.

8 Read the article again. Make notes about the things Luke writes about.

Who is involved	*Luke, his family and a local TV channel.*
What they did	
When they did it	
What happened	
What the consequences were	
What is happening next	

9 Imagine you are participating in a TV programme about saving energy. You are going to write an article about it for the school newspaper. Make notes for each heading in Exercise 8.

WRITE

10 Write your article. Look at page 93 of the Student's Book to help you.

_____
_____
_____
_____
_____
_____
_____
_____
_____
_____
_____
_____
_____
_____
_____
_____

CHECK

11 Check your writing. Can you say YES to these questions?

- Is the information from the list in Exercise 8 in your article?
- Have you used direct speech in your article?
- Have you used time linkers correctly?
- Have you used the active and passive correctly?
- Have you given the reader some background information?
- Are the spelling and punctuation correct?

Do you need to write a second draft?

Vocabulary
Materials

1 Complete the table with the words in the box.

> car tyres trumpets buildings T-shirts walls
> ~~windows~~ toys books pencils shoes

Glass	Plastic	Metal	Bricks	Wood
windows				
Cement	**Leather**	**Cotton**	**Rubber**	**Paper**

Total: 9

Energy issues

2 Complete the text with the words in the box.

> reduce ~~consume~~ turn waste
> save switch leave

People ¹ *consume* large amounts of energy every day. Sometimes they ² _____ energy when they ³ _____ their computers and TVs on standby all night. If you ⁴ _____ down the heating and ⁵ _____ off appliances when you don't need them, it will ⁶ _____ your energy bills. And it helps the planet to ⁷ _____ energy because there is less pollution.

Total: 6

Language focus
Present simple passive

3 Complete the text with the present passive form of the verbs in brackets.

We've got a very good recycling programme in our city – our waste ¹ ___*is not thrown*___ (not throw away). These blue bins ² _____ (collect) once a week. They ³ _____ (use) for paper and plastic. It ⁴ _____ (recycle) to make new paper and plastic. This green bin ⁵ _____ (not collect) every week – they only empty it every two weeks. It ⁶ _____ (use) for garden rubbish, like leaves. It ⁷ _____ (recycle) to make garden fertilizer. Some things, like phones and laptops ⁸ _____ (recycle), too. However, they ⁹ _____ (not collect) by the town council.

Total: 8

Past simple passive

4 Complete the text with the past simple passive form of the verbs in brackets. Add *by* where necessary.

This eco-house ¹ ___*was built*___ (build) in 1995. It ² _____ (design) Josie Jackman, an architect and 'eco warrior'. Solar panels ³ _____ (install) to provide all the energy for heating the house in winter. The walls ⁴ _____ (not make) from bricks, they ⁵ _____ (make) from recycled plastic and paper. The furniture ⁶ _____ (construct) Josie's husband, from recycled doors and windows. The roof ⁷ _____ (design) to catch rainwater to use inside the house. The house ⁸ _____ (not build) as a home, it ⁹ _____ (create) as an example of eco-friendly housing. Last year it ¹⁰ _____ (visit) over a hundred people.

Total: 9

Past simple passive questions

5 Complete the questions and answers about the text in Exercise 4.

1 When ___*was*___ the eco-house ___*built*___ ?
In 1995.

2 Who _____ the eco-house _____?
Josie Jackman.

3 Why _____ solar panels _____ ?
To provide energy for heating.

4 _____ the walls _____ from bricks?
No, _____ .

5 _____ the roof _____ to catch rainwater?
Yes, _____ .

6 How many people _____ the house _____ last year?
Over a hundred.

Total: 5

Language builder

6 Complete the conversation with the missing words. (Circle) the correct options.

> **A:** ¹___ my new T-shirt? It ²___ from recycled plastic bottles.
> **B:** That's amazing! I ³___ a T-shirt like that before.
> **A:** I ⁴___ it at an eco-shop in town. I ⁵___ it on Green Day next week.
> **B:** What's Green Day?
> **A:** It's one day a year when everyone ⁶___ do something green at school.
> **B:** That's a good idea. If people ⁷___ more to help the environment, we ⁸___ so many problems.
> **A:** Why don't you come? We ⁹___ great fun.
> **B:** I'm not sure. If I ¹⁰___ a lot of homework next week, I ¹¹___ to come to your school.
> **A:** Well, I hope you don't have ¹²___ homework then!

1	**a** Have you liked	**ⓑ** Do you like		**c** Were you liking
2	**a** 's made	**b** 're made		**c** 're make
3	**a** didn't see	**b** haven't seen		**c** don't see
4	**a** buy	**b** bought		**c** was buying
5	**a** 'll wear	**b** 'm going to wear		**c** wear
6	**a** have to	**b** has to		**c** had to
7	**a** were doing	**b** wouldn't do		**c** did
8	**a** don't have	**b** wouldn't have		**c** didn't have
9	**a** always have	**b** have always		**c** always has
10	**a** not have	**b** won't have		**c** don't have
11	**a** might try	**b** won't try		**c** might not try
12	**a** enough	**b** too much		**c** too many

Total: 11

Vocabulary builder

7 (Circle) the correct options.
1 Most of my T-shirts are made of ___ .
  a rubber **b** wood **ⓒ** cotton
2 Turn off the light to ___ energy.
  a save **b** reduce **c** consume
3 I only ___ in a test once and I felt awful!
  a screamed **b** handed **c** cheated
4 My mum doesn't know how to ___ a call on my mobile!
  a do **b** make **c** get
5 I don't like ___ . It's not nice to talk about other people.
  a arguing **b** whispering **c** gossiping
6 Ethan's leaving tomorrow but I don't know when he's ___ .
  a picking up **b** bringing down **c** coming back
7 Sometimes it's nice to have time ___ yourself.
  a by **b** on **c** of
8 Last week we went to see an orchestra at the concert ___ .
  a theatre **b** stage **c** hall
9 Before she left, she picked up her expensive red ___ bag.
  a plastic **b** leather **c** rubber
10 You ___ energy when appliances are on standby.
  a waste **b** reduce **c** save

Total: 9

Speaking

8 Complete the conversation with the words in the box.

> promise   the thing   meant   happened
> ~~mean~~   never   sorry   completely

> **A:** Where were you yesterday?
> **B:** What do you ¹____ _mean_ ____ ?
> **A:** I waited for you at the café for an hour.
> **B:** Oh no! I'm really ²_____ .
> I really ³_____ to come, honest!
> **A:** What ⁴_____ to you?
> **B:** Well, I ⁵_____ forgot.
> **A:** I called you but your phone was off.
> **B:** Yes, I know. ⁶_____ is, I had to stay late at school.
> **A:** Oh well, ⁷_____ mind. Let's go tomorrow.
> **B:** Great! I won't be late, I ⁸_____ !

Total: 7

Total: 64

Present simple passive

Remember that:
We use the present simple form of *be* + the past participle to form the present simple passive
✓ The houses are built from recycled materials.
✗ The houses ~~build~~ from recycled materials.
✗ The houses ~~built~~ from recycled materials.

1 Complete the sentences with the present simple passive form of the verb in brackets.

1 More than 60% of the rubbish in my town __is recycled__ (recycle).
2 Materials _____ (put) in different rubbish bins.
3 Bottles _____ (collect) in a large bin.
4 Old newspapers _____ (take) to the library for recycling.
5 Old clothes _____ (wash) and taken to special shops to be sold.
6 All of our rubbish _____ (reuse) if possible.

Passive review

2 Circle the correct options to complete the sentences.

1 Someone …
   a said me to go home and get some rest.
   b told me to go home and get some rest.
2 Rachel came in and …
   a asked me to help her clean the kitchen.
   b said me to help her clean the kitchen.
3 I told …
   a to come back tomorrow.
   b them to come back tomorrow.
4 They …
   a said us that they were going to a new school.
   b said that they were going to a new school.
5 We …
   a asked them to give us more time to finish the project.
   b said them to give us more time to finish the project.

the or no article?

Remember that:
- we always use *the* with countries that have *united* or *isles/islands* in their name, e.g. *the UK* and *the USA*. We don't use *the* with other country names.
  ✓ The USA has several renewable energy projects.
  ✗ ~~USA~~ has several renewable energy projects.
- we always use *the* when there is only one of the thing we are talking about, e.g. *the environment*
  ✓ Saving energy is important for the environment.
  ✗ Saving energy is important ~~for environment~~.
- we don't usually use *the* when we talk about things in a general way.
  ✓ Britain has got lots of sea and wind.
  ✗ Britain has got lots of ~~the~~ sea and wind.

3 Complete the sentences from Unit 8 with *the* or *X* (no article).

1 About a quarter of all the homes in ___X___ South Australia use solar power.
2 Colombia has many renewable sources that can be used to produce _____ energy.
3 In _____ UK it's not sunny very often.
4 Why is the sea so important for _____ planet?
5 _____ solar power isn't big in Britain.
6 _____ government is putting up wind farms.

Spell it right! Past participles

Remember that:
- with irregular verbs, the past simple form of the verb and the past participle are sometimes different.
  ✓ John fell (past simple) off his bike.
  ✓ John has fallen (past participle) off his bike.

4 Write the past simple and past participle form of the verbs from unit 8.

Infinitive	Past simple	Past participle
write	*wrote*	*written*
choose	_____	_____
grow	_____	_____
throw	_____	_____
show	_____	_____

Speaking extra

Giving your opinion

1 ★ ▶ **1.3** **Put the words in order to make sentences from the Real talk video in the Student's Book.**

1 cities / I / great / indoor / think / for / are / activities

_____

2 your / small / Everyone / town / knows / in / problems / a

_____

3 lot / in / country / a / There / shops / aren't / and concerts / of / the

_____

4 air / unhealthy / The / is / city / in / dirty and / the

_____

5 different / a / neighbourhood / You / go / park or / can / to / every day

_____

2 ★★ 🔊 **09** **Listen and choose the correct answer.**

Conversation 1:
1 The boy and girl live in the **city** / **country**.

Conversation 2:
2 The boy thinks he **has got** / **hasn't got** lots of friends.
3 The girl **agrees** / **doesn't agree** .

Conversation 3:
4 The girl goes to a **big** / **small** school.
5 Everybody laughed at him because he broke his **school bag** / **glasses**.

3 ★ **Read the conversation. Where does Amy want to live?**

Amy: I hate winter! It's freezing and there's another snow storm tomorrow.

Jamie: Yes, but at least our PE class will be indoors today.

Amy: I suppose **1**_____ . But it's so boring. We can't go anywhere.

Jamie: Maybe, **2**_____ where would you like to go?

Amy: To the beach. I **3**_____ life in California would be better. Why can't I live there? It'd be great to live in California.

Jamie: I don't **4**_____ . I like winter here. There's lots of snow and we can go skiing every day. It's great!

Amy: Well, I **5**_____ think so. You know I hate skiing. I'd prefer to be warm all the time, with sunny weather! Like in California.

Jamie: Perhaps **6**_____ right. But you'd have to put on sun cream all the time, carry a water bottle and wear sunglasses.

Amy: Yes! Great!

4 ★★ 🔊 **10** **Complete the conversation in Exercise 3 with the words in the box. Then listen and check.**

don't   so   you're   but   agree   reckon

Pronunciation focus: Agreeing and disagreeing

5 ★ 🔊 **11** **Where does the voice go up in these sentences? Listen and repeat.**

1 I think living in a warm country would be great.
2 I don't think I'd like to live in a cold country.
3 I reckon a big school is better.
4 I don't agree.
5 I think life would be great.

6 ★ 🔊 **12** **Listen to the conversation. What does Eva think is a good way to see the countryside?**

7 ★★★ 🔊 **12** **Listen again and complete the conversation.**

Nathan: I love going camping. **1**_____ it's great to sleep in a sleeping bag under the stars.

Eva: Camping? No, thanks. **2**_____ sleeping under the stars is great at all. You're probably freezing and in this country there's always heavy rain.

Nathan: That's **3**_____ . But where's your sense of adventure?

Eva: **4**_____ you have to be mad to go camping.

Nathan: **5**_____ it's the best way to see the countryside and to get some fresh air.

Eva: **6**_____. There are lots of ways to do that. You can go cycling or trekking. That's what I like doing.

Nathan: Yes, **7**_____ . But when you go camping, you have more time and it's more relaxing.

Eva: Fine, but I still prefer to sleep in a big comfortable bed in a hotel.

8 ★★ 🔊 **12** **Listen again and check your answers. Then listen and repeat the conversation.**

Speaking extra

Offering to help

1 ★ ▶ **2.3** **Match the sentence halves from the Real talk video in the Student's Book.**

1 It was an enormous job ___
2 A good friend doesn't have to do anything, ___
3 I'm not sad very often but when I am ___
4 I can't always talk to my parents. ___
5 Sometimes it's hard ___

a I only want to talk to my friend.
b It's easier to talk to my friend.
c but a real friend never lies to you.
d but fun doing it all together.
e they just have to be there.

2 ★★ 🔊 **13** **Listen and choose the correct answer.**

Conversation 1:
1 The girl is sending a message to say **hello** / **sorry** .
Conversation 2:
2 The girl is doing a **Maths** / **English** problem.
3 In the end she **understands** / **doesn't understand**.
Conversation 3:
4 The boy is doing a **History** / **Art** project.
5 He needs a photo of a **ship** / **computer** .

3 ★ **Read the conversation. Where do Lily and Chloe look for information first?**

Lily: Hey, Chloe. Can I ¹_____ you something?
Chloe: Yeah, sure. What's up?
Lily: It's this Social Science project. I have to write a biography of Nelson Mandela, but I'm not ²_____ where to start.
Chloe: He was very famous. What do you ³_____ ?
Lily: Well, where do I find out about him?
Chloe: I think you should look on the Internet first. Here, ⁴_____ me help you.
Lily: Thanks. That's really nice of you!
Chloe: It's easy. ⁵_____ you have to do is look at an online encyclopaedia. Read about him and make notes of the most important moments in his life.
Lily: I'm not very good at deciding what's important.
Chloe: Don't worry. I'll give you a ⁶_____ if you like.
Lily: Great! That's really kind.

4 ★★ 🔊 **14** **Complete the conversation in Exercise 3 with the words in the box. Then listen and check.**

| hand   sure   need   All   ask   let |

Pronunciation focus: Linking words

5 ★ 🔊 **15** **Listen to the sentences. Which words are linked? Listen and repeat.**

1 Can I ask you something?
2 I'll give you a hand.
3 Let me show you.
4 I'm not sure how to do it.
5 What do you need?

6 ★ 🔊 **16** **Listen to the conversation. What two things does Lewis want to know?**

7 ★★★ 🔊 **16** **Listen again and complete the conversation.**

Oliver: Hi Lewis? What are you doing?
Lewis: Oh, hi Oliver. Just some homework. But I'm so tired.
Oliver: Here, ¹_____ if you like.
Lewis: Thanks. I'm not very good at History.
Oliver: It's not that difficult. ²_____ is write the correct date.
Lewis: Yes, but I'm not very good at remembering dates. Especially when I'm tired!
Oliver: Yeah, I know. You forgot my birthday! ³_____ ?
Lewis: Let's see. When did the Romans come to Britain?
Oliver: That's in Chapter 1 of the History book. ⁴_____ .
Lewis: Thanks. Oliver, ⁵_____ something?
Oliver: Sure. What's up?
Lewis: How do I get a good night's sleep?
Oliver: You have to feel relaxed before you go to sleep.
Lewis: OK, but ⁶_____ do that.
Oliver: Well let's finish this History quiz first. Let's see … the Romans in Britain … Lewis? … Lewis?

8 ★★ 🔊 **16** **Listen again and check your answers. Then listen and repeat the conversation.**

Speaking extra

Invitations and arrangements

1 ★ ▶ **3.3** **Complete the sentences from the Real talk video in the Student's Book with the words in the box.**

> birthday   years   crowd   cheaper   people

1 I love being part of a _____ .
2 I don't like listening to music with a lot of _____ around.
3 I went to my first one when I was only five _____ old.
4 I saw One Direction for my _____ last year and they were amazing.
5 Cinema tickets are _____ than concert tickets.

2 ★★ 🔊 **17** **Listen and write the answers.**
Conversation 1:
1 What's the photo exhibition about?

_____

Conversation 2:
2 What are the girls talking about?

_____

3 Where are they going to meet?

_____

Conversation 3:
4 What kind of festival is it?

_____

5 How are the boys going to get there?

_____

3 ★ **Read the conversation. When are Will and Carol going to buy concert tickets?**

Will:	Oh, look, The King Birds are coming to do a concert.
Carol:	Great! Do you ¹_____ going to see them?
Will:	Yeah, why not? ²_____ I ask my dad to get tickets?
Carol:	No, let's go and buy them ³_____ .
Will:	⁴_____ good.
Carol:	Where are they selling them?
Will:	In *Piano Sounds* – that shop in town.
Carol:	How ⁵_____ going this afternoon?
Will:	OK, what time shall we meet?
Carol:	After school?
Will:	That's a great ⁶_____ ! See you later.

4 ★★ 🔊 **18** **Complete the conversation in Exercise 3 with the words in the box. Then listen and check your answers.**

> about   Shall   together   Sounds   idea   fancy

Pronunciation focus: Invitations

5 ★ 🔊 **19** **Listen to the invitations. Does the voice go up or down? Listen and repeat.**
1 Do you fancy going to a concert?
2 Shall I ask Rebecca to come with us?
3 How about going after school?
4 Shall I go to your house?
5 How about going for an ice cream later?

6 ★ 🔊 **20** **Listen to the conversation. Where are Liam and Connor going to practise?**

7 ★★★ 🔊 **20** **Listen again and complete the conversation.**

Connor:	Hey, Liam, you play the guitar, don't you?
Liam:	Yes, I do.
Connor:	Well, I play the drums. ¹_____ playing together?
Liam:	Yeah, ²_____ ? Can we practise at your house?
Connor:	I think so. I'll have to check with my parents.
Liam:	³_____ Helen to come, too? She plays the piano and her friend Florence plays the bass guitar.
Connor:	That's ⁴_____ ! We can all practise together.
Liam:	Hey, ⁵_____ starting a band?
Connor:	Well, let's practise together first.
Liam:	What time shall ⁶_____ ?
Connor:	I'll talk to my parents and then I'll send you a message.
Liam:	⁷_____ ! I'll start thinking of a band name. Liam and Friends? One Liam? Liam and the Gang? …

8 ★★ 🔊 **20** **Listen again and check your answers. Then listen and repeat the conversation.**

Speaking extra

Signing up for an activity

1 ★ ▶ **4.3** **Complete the sentences from the Real talk video in the Student's Book with the words in the box.**

> nervous   times   scary   awesome   cold

1 It was really good fun but _____ at the same time.

2 It was so loud and really _____ . It was July so I didn't expect that.

3 I was always too scared but last year I jumped. It was _____ .

4 I was really _____ before I started.

5 I've been on the biggest roller coaster in the world five _____ .

2 ★★ 🔊 **21** **Listen and choose the correct words.**

Conversation 1:

1 The boy is going to do a **skiing / sailing** course.

Conversation 2:

2 The girl is going **climbing / trekking**.

3 The boy should wear **sun cream / sunglasses**.

Conversation 3:

4 The girl is going **climbing / whitewater rafting**.

5 They're going to go **on foot / by bus**.

3 ★ **Read the conversation. How long will Justin be at the theme park?**

Justin:	Can I ¹_____ you a few things about the trip to the theme park?
Guide:	Sure. What ²_____ you like to know?
Justin:	First of all, what time are we leaving tomorrow?
Guide:	The bus leaves at 10 o'clock in the morning and you'll be back here at about five o'clock.
Justin:	So how ³_____ is the journey to the theme park?
Guide:	It's not far, about 40 minutes.
Justin:	OK, what do we need to ⁴_____ ?
Guide:	Nothing really. Maybe some money for water or sweets, but lunch is included.
Justin:	Does the price ⁵_____ all the different rides?
Guide:	Yes, you can go on everything.
Justin:	Even the *Monster Mountain* roller coaster?
Guide:	Everything.
Justin:	OK, where can I ⁶_____ up?
Guide:	Right here. What's your name? …

4 ★★ 🔊 **22** **Complete the conversation in Exercise 3 with the words in the box. Then listen and check.**

> include   long   would   sign   bring   ask

Pronunciation focus: Asking for information

5 ★ 🔊 **23** **Listen to the questions. Does the voice go up or down? Listen and repeat.**

1 Where can I sign up?

2 What about food?

3 Can I ask you a few things about the course?

4 Does the price include transport?

5 How long is the trip?

6 What do I need to bring?

6 ★ 🔊 **24** **Listen to the conversation. Why is Taylor surprised?**

7 ★★★ 🔊 **24** **Listen again and complete the conversation.**

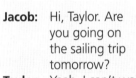

Jacob:	Hi, Taylor. Are you going on the sailing trip tomorrow?
Taylor:	Yeah. I can't wait. This is my third time! Are you going too?
Jacob:	I don't know. I've never been sailing. ¹_____ a few things about the trip?
Taylor:	Sure.
Jacob:	²_____ ? I mean how long are we out in the boats?
Taylor:	Oh, we're usually out for about three or four hours.
Jacob:	OK, wow! That's a long time … and ³_____ ?
Taylor:	Well, swim shorts, shoes that you can get wet … and that's all I think.
Jacob:	⁴_____ life jackets?
Taylor:	Oh, no. You'll get one of those.
Jacob:	And ⁵_____ some swimming lessons first?
Taylor:	Swimming lessons? Err …no. You can't swim?
Jacob:	Well, no.

8 ★★ 🔊 **24** **Listen again and check your answers. Then listen and repeat the conversation.**

Speaking extra

Reassuring someone

1 ★ ▶ **5.3** **Match the sentence halves from the Real talk video in the Student's Book.**

1 I had a lot of photos _____
2 I haven't yet but _____
3 I had to talk for two minutes _____
4 My friend and I did _____

a I'm doing one next week.
b about my family and friends.
c a presentation about our summer camp last year.
d so the class loved it (my presentation).

2 ★★ 🔊 **25** **Listen and answer the questions.**
Conversation 1:

1 How long has the girl practised the piano for?
_____

Conversation 2:

2 What has the teacher asked everyone to do?
_____

3 What's the boy's problem?
_____

Conversation 3:

4 What's happening tomorrow?
_____

5 Who can't play?
_____

3 ★ **Read the conversation. Why are Lucy and James going shopping?**

Lucy: Oh, you're so lucky you're going to Berlin tomorrow on the school exchange! Are you excited?
James: Yes, but I'm also a bit worried.
Lucy: Don't ¹_____ . It'll be fine.
James: Yes, but what if I don't like my exchange student?
Lucy: No ²_____ . I'm sure you'll like him.
James: And what if he doesn't like me?
Lucy: You'll be ³_____ . You're a really nice person.
James: And I can't speak German – I don't know what to say.
Lucy: Of ⁴_____ you can. You're the best in the class.
James: And I haven't got a present for my exchange student's family.
Lucy: I think I can ⁵_____ you. Come on, let's go shopping.
James: Thanks, Lucy. I just can't think of anything to get them.
Lucy: No problem… it doesn't have to be a big present. It'll ⁶_____ out all right.

4 ★★ 🔊 **26** **Complete the conversation in Exercise 3 with the words in the box. Then listen and check your answers.**

| help   fine   turn   worry   problem   course |

Pronunciation focus: Giving instructions

5 ★ 🔊 **27** **Listen to the instructions. Does the voice go up and then down or down and then up? Listen and repeat.**

1 Don't worry!
2 You'll be fine.
3 No problem.
4 You don't need to worry.
5 Of course you can.

6 ★ 🔊 **28** **Listen to the conversation. Why is Jake very nervous?**

7 ★★★ 🔊 **28** **Listen again and complete the conversation.**

Tom: So are you going to call her or not?
Jake: Yes… just hold on. I don't know what to say.
Tom: ¹_____ . Just say hello.
Jake: OK … Hello, Jessica … and then what?
Tom: ²_____ help you. What do you want to say to her?
Jake: I want to ask her to help me with this project. But I can't do it!
Tom: ³_____ . Just say hello and then ask her to help you.
Jake: But what if she says no? She might laugh at me.
Tom: No, she won't. ⁴_____ . Just call her.
Jake: OK … can't I just send her a text message?
Tom: No, it's better if you call her. ⁵_____ .
Jake: I'm really nervous.
Tom: ⁶_____ . She'll help you. I know she will!

8 ★★ 🔊 **28** **Listen again and check your answers. Then listen and repeat the conversation.**

Speaking extra

Expressing surprise

1 ★ ▶ **6.3** **Complete the sentences from the Real talk video in the Student's Book with the words in the box.**

> real   music   everywhere   eyes   brother   terrified

1   I'm in a room and there are hundreds of spiders and thousands of snakes _____ .
2   When I was little, my _____ locked me in a closet for two hours.
3   I'm terrified of crocodiles but I've never seen a _____ one.
4   I always close my _____ when we take off and I listen to _____ .
5   I don't have any big fears but my dad's _____ of me.

2 ★★ 🔊 **29** **Listen and answer the questions.**

Conversation 1:
1   What's on the fourth floor?
_____

Conversation 2:
2   Where was the boy yesterday?
_____

3   Who was his best friend?
_____

Conversation 3:
4   What do the girl's parents want to do?
_____

5   What instrument would the girl like to learn?
_____

3 ★ **Read the conversation. Where are Oliver and Alice?**

Oliver: Where are we going now?
Alice: Well, we've seen the elephants, the lions, and the snakes – ugh! We're going to see the birds next.
Oliver: Birds? No thanks. I'm terrified of birds.
Alice: Are you ¹_____ ?
Oliver: Yeah … well, I just don't like them.
Alice: That's ²_____ . Birds aren't dangerous.
Oliver: Yeah … I know, but …
Alice: I don't ³_____ you! Anyway, the birds are in a zoo – they can't go near you.
Oliver: I don't care. They're too close for me.
Alice: Oh, come on. You're ⁴_____ .
Oliver: Look … it's quite common.
Alice: That can't be ⁵_____ !
Oliver: It is true. People are afraid of dogs, insects, spiders … why not birds?
Alice: What? No ⁶_____ !

4 ★★ 🔊 **30** **Complete the conversation in Exercise 3 with the words in the box. Then listen and check.**

> true   serious   way   believe   impossible   joking

Pronunciation focus: Sounding surprised

5 ★ 🔊 **31** **Listen and repeat the sentences.**
1   No way!
2   You're joking.
3   That can't be true.
4   That's impossible.
5   I don't believe you.

6 ★ 🔊 **32** **Listen to the conversation. What happened to the unluckiest man in the world's house?**

7 ★★★ 🔊 **32** **Listen again and complete the conversation.**

Lily: Wow! What a story! I'm reading about the unluckiest man in the world.
Simon: Oh, yeah. Why is he so unlucky?
Lily: Well, he fell on a skiing trip in Colorado.
Simon: OK, that's quite common.
Lily: Yes, but there was a snowstorm so the helicopter couldn't take him to the hospital so he had to lie in the snow for four hours.
Simon: ¹_____ ?
Lily: Anyway, they took him to hospital and fixed his leg and sent him home. And then he fell again and broke his other leg!
Simon: What? ²_____ !
Lily: So after that, while he was at home with his two broken legs, a snake came into the house and bit him.
Simon: A snake? ³_____ !
Lily: So they took him to hospital but he got trapped in the lift.
Simon: ⁴_____ !
Lily: Anyway, he got out of the lift, saw the doctor and while he was still in hospital, there was a fire at his house.
Simon: ⁵_____ !
Lily: His house was completely destroyed and he lost everything he had!
Simon: ⁶_____ .
Lily: No, it isn't actually. It's not true at all. But you'd believe anything!

8 ★★ 🔊 **32** **Listen again and check your answers. Then listen and repeat the conversation.**

Speaking extra

Asking for and giving advice

1 ★ ▶ **7.3** **Complete the sentences from the Real talk video in the Student's Book with the words in the box.**

> better   advice   helps   problems   wise

1 When I have _____ with my friends she always says the right thing.
2 He _____ me with everything.
3 She always gives me good _____ .
4 She always makes me feel _____ .
5 She's lived a long time so she's very _____ .

2 ★★ 🔊 **33** **Listen and answer the questions.**

Conversation 1:
1 What advice does the boy give?
_____

Conversation 2:
2 When's the detention?
_____

3 What's the girl doing this weekend?
_____

Conversation 3:
4 What's in the first message Nathan received?
_____

5 Whose phone number is it?
_____

3 ★ **Read the conversation. Did something good or bad happen to Natasha?**

John:	Hi, Natasha. You look worried. What's the ¹_____ ?
Natasha:	Well … I need your ²_____ . A friend of mine posted a horrible photo of me on Facebook and she didn't ask me first.
John:	Well, it's always a good ³_____ to ask the person's permission, isn't it?
Natasha:	Exactly. And now her friends are making comments about me. What do you think I ⁴_____ do?
John:	Well, if I were you, I ⁵_____ reply to any of the comments.
Natasha:	Yes, but some of them aren't very nice. My parents say I shouldn't ⁶_____ but they don't understand.
John:	Have you ⁷_____ asking your friend to take the photo off Facebook? Maybe we could talk to her ⁸_____ .
Natasha:	Thanks, John.

4 ★★ 🔊 **34** **Complete the conversation in Exercise 4 with the words in the box. Then listen and check your answers.**

> tried   wouldn't   idea   problem
> worry   advice   together   should

Pronunciation focus: Sentence stress

5 ★ 🔊 **35** **Listen. <u>Underline</u> the stressed words in the sentences. Listen and repeat.**

1 I need your advice.
2 If I were you, I'd ask her.
3 Maybe we could go together.
4 Have you tried calling her?
5 It's a good idea to call first.

6 ★ 🔊 **36** **Listen to the conversation. How do Emily and Tania decide to help each other?**

7 ★★★ 🔊 **36** **Listen again and complete the conversation.**

Emily:	Tania, ¹_____ .
Tania:	²_____ , Emily?
Emily:	It's my Maths grade. It's awful. I have to get better grades. What do you think ³_____ ?
Tania:	Well, first of all ⁴_____ organise your notes. You should write things down and look at them at home.
Emily:	Yes, but I don't understand anything in class.
Tania:	⁵_____ talking to the teacher?
Emily:	Mr Banks? Yes, he tries to help me but …
Tania:	I'm the same in Music. You've heard me on the piano. I'm terrible. I've talked to my parents but they're so happy with my marks in Maths …
Emily:	Oh, but Music is so easy. ⁶_____ spend more time on your Music and less time on Maths. So what did your parents say?
Tania:	They said ⁷_____ but I really want to be able to play the piano better.
Emily:	Hey! I've got an idea. ⁸_____ work together. You help me with Maths and I'll help you with the piano.
Tania:	That's a fantastic idea. Let's start now. Listen to this …

8 ★★ 🔊 **36** **Listen again and check your answers. Then listen and repeat the conversation.**

Speaking extra

Apologising and explaining

1 ★ ▶️ 8.3 **Complete the sentences from the Real talk video in the Student's Book with the verbs in the box.**

> animals   litter   watering plants
> community centre   babysit

1 My friend reads to older people at the
   _____ once a month.
2 I'm not sure but I know you can help older people
   with their _____ .
3 You can pick up _____ in the park with
   the Scouts.
4 I _____ for my little brother all the time
   and I don't get money for it.
5 You can help in the garden doing things like
   _____ .

2 ★★ 🔊 37 **Listen and answer the questions.**
Conversation 1:
1 What does the teacher want?
   _____

Conversation 2:
2 What was on at the gallery?
   _____

3 Why didn't the girl go?
   _____

Conversation 3:
4 What was Joe fixing?
   _____

5 How long did Joe wait for Ben?
   _____

3 ★ **Read the conversation. Where did Olivia go yesterday? Why didn't Ruby come?**

Olivia:	Hi Ruby. What happened to you yesterday?
Ruby:	Oh, I'm ¹_____ sorry. You went to the park with Scouts to pick up litter, didn't you?
Olivia:	Yes, and you didn't come. What happened?
Ruby:	Yeah, I'm ²_____ . I really ³_____ to come, honest!
Olivia:	Did you fall asleep?
Ruby:	No, the ⁴_____ is, my mum's painting my room and I had to tidy it first.
Olivia:	But why didn't you send me a message?
Ruby:	I completely ⁵_____ . I started tidying … and the ⁶_____ was I just didn't see the time.
Olivia:	Oh well, never ⁷_____ . We're going again next week.
Ruby:	Oh, great. I'll come next week, I ⁸_____ .

4 ★★ 🔊 38 **Complete the conversation in Exercise 3 with the words in the box. Then listen and check.**

> forgot   really   mind   sorry   thing
> meant   promise   problem

Pronunciation focus: Apologising

5 ★ 🔊 39 **Listen to the apologies. Does the voice go up or down? Listen and repeat.**
1 I'm sorry.
2 I'm really sorry.
3 I meant to come.
4 I completely forgot.
5 I'll come next time, I promise.

6 ★ 🔊 40 **Listen to the conversation. What did David want Julia to help him with yesterday?**

7 ★★★ 🔊 40 **Listen again and complete the conversation.**

David:	Oh, hi Julia. Where were you yesterday? I had to do my French homework. I asked you to come and help me.
Julia:	¹_____ , David. Have you finished it?
David:	Yes, and I've given it to the teacher.
Julia:	²_____ , honest. I know it was really important.
David:	Yes, it was.
Julia:	³_____ . I wanted to do it with you. ⁴_____ , I had to help my dad in the garden.
David:	I sent you text message. Why didn't you answer it?
Julia:	I saw it but ⁵_____ , right at that moment my dad was cutting down a tree and then ⁶_____ .
David:	⁷_____ . So will you help me with my next French homework?
Julia:	More French homework? Well, the thing is … I'm really sorry, but …
David:	What now?
Julia:	Of course, I'll help you, David … tomorrow. ⁸_____ .
David:	Tomorrow? But I have to do it now! Oh come on, Julia …

8 ★★ 🔊 40 **Listen again and check your answers. Then listen and repeat the conversation.**

Language focus extra

Wh- questions

1 Complete the mini-conversations with the words in the box.

> Where ~~How old~~ Whose
> How When What Who

1 **A:** _____How old_____ is your dad?
  B: He's thirty-nine.
2 **A:** _____ do you walk to school with?
  B: My sister.
3 **A:** _____ did you have lunch yesterday?
  B: In the school café.
4 **A:** _____ bicycle is that?
  B: I think it's Sara's.
5 **A:** _____ are you?
  B: Fine, thanks.
6 **A:** _____ is the first thing you do when you get up?
  B: I have a shower.
7 **A:** _____ do you usually do your homework?
  B: In the morning before school!

Adjectives and adverbs

2 Complete the sentences with the correct form of the adjective or adverb.

1 *careful*
  A: Please be _____careful_____ when you ride to school.
  B: Don't worry. I always ride _____carefully_____ .
2 *quick*
  A: We need to walk more _____ or we'll be late.
  B: I'm sorry, I'm not a _____ walker.
3 *easy*
  A: That was an _____ test, wasn't it?
  B: Yes, I think everyone passed it _____ .
4 *good*
  A: Sam sings really _____ doesn't she?
  B: Yes, she's a really _____ singer.

Comparative and superlative adjectives

3 Circle the correct options.

1 My sister is **older** / **the oldest** than me.
2 Driving is **dangerouser** / **more dangerous** than flying.
3 This is the **worse** / **worst** holiday of my life!

4 I've got long hair, but Anna's hair is **more long** / **longer** .
5 You are the **more** / **most** intelligent person in the class.
6 It's the **most funny** / **funniest** film that I've got on DVD.

Comparative and superlative adverbs

4 Rewrite the sentences. Use a comparative or superlative adverb.

1 Dan is a slower runner than me.
  Dan runs *more slowly than me* _____ .
2 You are a better dancer than Jill.
  You dance _____ .
3 Bella is a more careful writer than the other students.
  Bella writes _____ .
4 I'm a quieter speaker than most people.
  I speak _____ .
5 Tom is the most dangerous driver in my family.
  Tom drives _____ .
6 You are the quickest reader.
  You read _____ .

Past simple

5 Complete the text with the past simple form of the verbs in brackets.

Last Saturday I **1**_____was_____ (be) at my friend Susan's thirteenth birthday. She **2**_____ (have) a party at her house, and lots of people **3**_____ (come). It **4**_____ (start) at 8pm. I **5**_____ (see) some friends there and we **6**_____ (talk) and **7**_____ (laugh) for hours. We also **8**_____ (dance) and **9**_____ (eat) lots of cake. I **10**_____ (not want) the party to end!

6 Put the words in the correct order.

1 an / breakfast / ate / I / ago / hour
  I ate breakfast an hour ago. _____
2 week / last / party / had /a / Julia
  _____
3 do / last / did / night / What / you?
  _____
4 ill / felt / morning / I / yesterday
  _____
5 me / call / you / night / didn't / last / Why?
  _____
6 ago / I / film / this / saw / months / three
  _____

Language focus extra

Present simple and continuous

1 Circle the correct options.

1 I don't want to go outside. It rains / **'s raining** .

2 Do you walk / Are you walking to school every day?

3 I usually **eat** / am eating some fruit after lunch.

4 Do you watch / Are you watching the football match? It's really boring.

5 Emily can't come with us. She does / **'s doing** her homework.

6 I **don't usually go** / 'm not usually going to bed until 11 o'clock.

7 Look! The baby dances / is dancing. Take a photo.

8 We don't go / **'re not going** shopping now. There's a snowstorm outside!

2 Complete the conversation. Use the present simple or the present continuous form of the verbs in brackets.

John: Hello. ¹ _Are you doing_ (you do) anything special at the moment?

Katie: Right now, I ² _____ (look after) my little brother. Why?

John: What time ³ _____ (your mum get) home from work?

Katie: She ⁴ _____ (work) late every Thursday, so at about half past eight. Why?

John: They ⁵ _____ (show) the new Miley Cyrus film at the cinema on Main Street. My sister and I ⁶ _____ (think) about going. ⁷ _____ (you want) to come with us?

Katie: Yes, please! Let's meet at the cinema at quarter to nine!

John: Great. It ⁸ _____ (rain) so take an umbrella.

Past simple and past continuous

3 Circle the correct options.

1 I didn't hear that the teacher talked / **was talking** to me.

2 Dan was sending / **sent** me a text when I was playing tennis.

3 On holiday, we **went** / were going swimming every day.

4 We were listening / **listened** to loud music, but my dad told us to turn it down.

5 My mum **made** / was making lunch when I got home.

6 When I was young, we were visiting / **visited** my grandparents every weekend.

7 I washed / **was washing** my dad's car when it started to rain.

8 Did you watch / **Were you watching** the end of the film last night? What happened?

9 When you called Eva, she played / **was playing** the guitar.

10 After the basketball match, I had / **was having** a shower and went home.

4 Complete the sentences. Use the past simple or past continuous form of the verbs in brackets.

a When I ¹ _arrived_ (arrive) home after school yesterday, my family was very busy! My mum ² _____ (work), my brother ³ _____ (do) his homework and my sister ⁴ _____ (practise) the piano.

b Yesterday I ⁵ _____ (have) a shower when suddenly, I ⁶ _____ (hear) a strange noise coming from downstairs. I ⁷ _____ (get) out of the shower, ⁸ _____ (go) downstairs and then I ⁹ _____ (see) my cat with a mouse in his mouth!

5 Complete the text. Use the past simple or the past continuous form of the verbs in brackets.

When I woke up, it ¹ _was raining_ (rain). I ² _____ (walk) to the bathroom, but my brother ³ _____ (have) a shower. I ⁴ _____ (tell) him to be quick, and then I ⁵ _____ (go) to the kitchen. Dad ⁶ _____ (read) the newspaper, and Mum ⁷ _____ (listen) to the radio.

'⁸ _____ (you sleep) well?' asked Dad.

'No,' I said, 'I ⁹ _____ (have) a very strange dream about my English class. I ¹⁰ _____ (sit) at my desk when the teacher ¹¹ _____ (ask) me a question.'

'That's not very strange,' my mum said.

'Yes, but when I ¹² _____ (answer) the question, I ¹³ _____ (speak) really quietly and the teacher ¹⁴ _____ (not hear) me. Everyone ¹⁵ _____ (laugh) and then I ¹⁶ _____ (wake up)!'

Language focus extra

should

1 Two friends are planning a party.
Write sentences and questions with *should*.
Add extra words if necessary.

1 we / ask your parents for permission?
' *Should we ask your parents for permission?* '
'I asked them yesterday.'

2 we / invite?
'_____'
'Everyone in the class.'

3 they / bring some food and drink?
'_____'
'No, my mum is going to get everything.'

4 everyone / arrive / 8 pm. Is that OK?
'_____'
'Yes, about 8 pm is fine.'

5 I / wear?
'_____'
'Your blue skirt and white T-shirt.'

6 I / bring some dance music. What do you think?
'_____'
'Yes, that's a good idea.'

must

2 Complete the sentences with *must* or *mustn't*.

1 You _____*mustn't*_____ forget to call me tonight.

2 Students _____ write in pen, not pencil.

3 You _____ tell anyone. It's a secret.

4 Tell them that they _____ relax more.
It's OK.

5 We _____ make a lot of noise. This is
the library.

6 I _____ be late, because Dad gets
angry.

3 Circle the correct options.

1 You **shouldn't** / **must** be scared to follow your
dreams.

2 You **should** / **shouldn't** make promises you can't
keep.

3 You're always tired. You really **should** / **mustn't**
get more sleep.

4 You **must** / **should** listen more, and speak less.

5 You **must** / **mustn't** criticise other people. It's not
nice.

6 You **must** / **shouldn't** wear your glasses. You
can't see without them!

7 You **shouldn't** / **must** give up. Try again!

8 You **mustn't** / **shouldn't** drink that water. It'll
make you sick.

9 You **must** / **should** do something creative if
you're bored.

have to / don't have to

4 Complete the sentences and questions with
the correct form of *have to*.

1 You _*don't have to*_ phone. You can email for
information.

2 At my school, we _____ play hockey,
but there is a school team.

3 Doctors _____ study for seven or eight
years.

4 Why _____ (she) do the exam again?

5 My brother _____ study much.
He's really clever.

6 _____ (we) take a sleeping bag with
us?

7 I _____ help around the house but
I don't mind.

8 It's OK. You _____ speak quietly.
The baby woke up a few minutes ago.

5 Complete the sentences with *don't have to* or
mustn't and the verbs in the box.

```
have   go   use   do   play
speak   forget   watch
```

1 You _*mustn't use*_ your mobile phone. It's not
allowed.

2 You _____ your homework now.
You can do it later.

3 We _____ a film. We can go out if you
like.

4 You _____ your first aid kit when you
go camping.

5 You _____ a snack now. We're going to
have dinner in 10 minutes.

6 We _____ to school today. It's a holiday.

7 It's OK. You _____ slowly. I understand
you.

8 It's 1 o'clock in the morning. You _____
your guitar now. Go to sleep!

Language focus extra

Present perfect for indefinite past time

1 Write the past participle form of these irregular verbs. Then write the infinitive form of the irregular past participles.

1 speak	_spoken_	**9** gone	_go_	
2 be	_____	**10** done	_____	
3 take	_____	**11** sung	_____	
4 see	_____	**12** got	_____	
5 come	_____	**13** made	_____	
6 feel	_____	**14** given	_____	
7 meet	_____	**15** won	_____	
8 write	_____	**16** eaten	_____	

2 Complete the sentences. Use the present perfect form of the verbs in brackets.

1 I _'ve finished_ washing the car. (finish)

2 We _____ a window because it is really hot today. (open)

3 Your birthday card from Uncle David _____. (not arrive)

4 You _____ the shopping into the kitchen. (not carry)

5 They _____ visiting the museums and art galleries this weekend. (enjoy)

6 She _____ Leo four times this week. (email)

7 You _____ very well. You've got 10 points. (do)

8 He _____ the most beautiful portrait. Come and see it. (paint)

3 Circle the correct options.

1 My mum's not here. She's **gone** / **been** to the shops.

2 I've never **gone** / **been** to this gallery before. It's amazing.

3 He's **gone** / **been** on stage many times. He loves acting.

4 Keely's **gone** / **been** to Spain. I hope the weather's nice while she's there.

5 I've **gone** / **been** shopping on this street before.

6 They've **gone** / **been** cycling. They'll be back soon.

Present perfect – questions

4 Look at the table. Write present perfect questions with *ever* and the correct answers. ✓ = yes and ✗ = no.

	Charlotte	Aiden and Milo	You
Climb a mountain	¹✓	³✗	⁵?
Win a prize	²✗	⁴✓	⁶?

1 _Has Charlotte ever climbed a mountain?_
   Yes, she has.

2 _____

3 _____

4 _____

5 _____

6 _____

5 Complete the questions with the correct form of the present perfect. Then match the questions with the answers.

1 ___*Have you ever made*___ (you / ever / make) dinner for your family?   _c_

2 _____ (you / ever / do) karaoke?   ____

3 How many different countries _____ (you / go) to?   ____

4 _____ (your grandmother / ever / send) you an email?   ____

5 Where _____ (your brothers / go)?   ____

6 Which of these DVDs _____ (you / see)?   ____

a Just three. Ireland, France and Japan.

b They've gone camping for the weekend.

c Yes, I have. I love cooking.

d No, I haven't. I don't like singing in front of people.

e I haven't seen any of them, I think.

f Yes, she has. She's really good at using computers.

Language focus extra

Present perfect with *still*, *yet*, *already* and *just*

1 Complete the sentences with *still*, *yet*, *already* or *just*.

1 You _____still_____ haven't bought me a birthday present.

2 I haven't seen the new Superman film _____ .

3 I've _____ tidied my room, so don't touch anything!

4 Harry's _____ broken his new computer. He's only had it for two weeks!

5 They haven't asked their parents for permission _____ .

6 Sorry, but I've _____ made plans for this weekend.

7 I've _____ found out that we're going skiing next month! I'm so excited!

8 Lucy _____ hasn't decided what she wants to do at university.

2 Put the words in the correct order to make sentences.

1 already / the news / have / I / heard
I have already heard the news.

2 tidied / yet / you / Have / your bedroom / ?
_____

3 me / hasn't / She / phoned / still
_____

4 just / hungry / I'm / dinner / I've / not / because / had
_____

5 home / already / He / has / gone
_____

6 arrived / still / haven't / They
_____

7 heard / amazing / just / I've / busker / an
_____

8 yet / he / the book / read / Has / ?
_____

Present perfect with *for* and *since*

3 Complete the table with the words in the box.

| three weeks   Monday   2008   Christmas |
| a long time   two hours |

for	since
three weeks	

4 Circle the correct options.

1 I've had my mobile **for** / since a year.

2 We've been here **for** / **since** this morning.

3 She hasn't spoken to me **for** / **since** months.

4 It hasn't rained **for** / **since** April.

5 Laura's been my friend **for** / **since** we were six.

6 They haven't seen each other **for** / **since** twelve weeks.

Present perfect and past simple

5 Circle the correct options.

1 ___ out with your friends last weekend?
   a Have you gone   **b** Did you go

2 I ___ when we went to the beach.
   a 've been happy   **b** was happy

3 ___ in Spain all your life?
   a Have you lived   **b** Did you live

4 Eric ___ golf before.
   a has never played   **b** never played

5 She still ___ the monkeys.
   a hasn't seen   **b** didn't see

6 I ___ you like painting.
   a haven't known   **b** didn't know

6 Complete the conversation. Use the present perfect or the past simple form of the verbs in brackets.

Mum:	Sam, [1] *Have you seen* (you see) Julia?
Sam:	No, I [2]_____ (see) her since last night. We [3]_____ (watch) TV when she came home. She was tired, so she [4]_____ (go) to bed early. Why?
Mum:	She isn't here, and she [5]_____ (not go) to school. Her teacher [6]_____ (just call).
Sam:	I don't know. [7]_____ (you ask) Dad?
Mum:	I rang the office, but he [8]_____ (still not reply) to my message.
Julia:	Hi!
Mum:	Julia! Where [9]_____ (you be)?
Julia:	Sorry, Mum. I [10]_____ (take) the bus to school but I [11]_____ (come back) because I [12]_____ (not feel) very well. I [13]_____ (just/take) some medicine.
Mum:	[14]_____ (you have) breakfast yet?
Julia:	Yes, I have. I'm going back to bed.

Language focus extra

will, *might*, *may* + adverbs of possibility

1 Complete the mini-conversations with *will/won't* or *might/might not* and the verb phrases in the box.

> be   play for the team   call me   understand
> ~~pass easily~~   love it   find the way

1 **A:** I'm worried about the exam.
   B: Don't worry! You*'ll pass easily* .

2 **A:** I hope Sally doesn't get lost.
   B: It's okay. She _____ because she's got a map.

3 **A:** I've bought Luke and Harry a birthday present.
   B: I'm sure they _____ .

4 **A:** David didn't score any goals in the match yesterday.
   B: I know. He _____ next year.

5 **A:** I'm nervous about telling Dad I broke his MP3 player.
   B: Don't worry! He _____ it was an accident.

6 **A:** What instrument is that busker playing?
   B: I don't know. I think it _____ a clarinet.

7 **A:** Is Kate coming to the cinema tonight?
   B: She doesn't know. She's very busy. She _____ later.

2 Complete the mini-conversations with *will/won't* or *might/might not* and the ideas in brackets.

1 **A:** What are you doing this weekend?
   B: I'm not sure. _I might go skateboarding_ . (go skateboarding)

2 **A:** Where are you going to meet Megan?
   B: We haven't decided. We _____ . (at the train station)

3 **A:** When is Paula going to see Eric?
   B: I think she _____ . (on Thursday)

4 **A:** Are you coming to the football match tonight?
   B: I can't, but I _____ . (watch it on TV)

5 **A:** Are you going to email me tonight?
   B: Yes, and I _____ (tell) you all the gossip about school!

6 **A:** Can your mum cut my hair this weekend?
   B: She's working, so she _____ . (not have time)

7 **A:** Can I go to your house tonight?'
   B: No, I've got a piano lesson so I _____ . (be at home)

3 ⊙Circle the correct options.

1 I'll (probably) / certainly buy the red one, but I'm going to think about it.

2 She'll **definitely** / **probably** be late. She always is!

3 We **definitely will** / **'ll definitely** do it.

4 They **will probably** / **certainly will** need help.

5 He **probably** / **definitely** won't know, but ask!

6 Computers **will certainly** / **definitely will** take over the world – the question is when!

First conditional + *may/might*, *be able to*

4 Write sentences in the first conditional.

1 I / angry / criticise / If / might / him, / he / be
   If I criticise him, he might be angry.

2 won't / I / lend / me / her / She / probably / if / ask / her book
   _____

3 my blog / you / might / put it on / If / me / the photo, / send / I
   _____

4 won't / do / that / have / you / any friends / You / if
   _____

5 embarrassed / her / ask / be / you / She / might / if
   _____

6 you / be able to / go home / If / now / you'll / your homework / do
   _____

5 Complete the sentences with the correct form of the verb phrases in the box.

> not listen carefully   not speak loudly   hold his hand
> tell him to call you   ~~go to the park~~
> send you a friend request   not remind them

1 If it's sunny tomorrow, we'll _go to the park_ .

2 If we see him, we _____ _____ .

3 You won't understand if you _____ _____ .

4 He might not be frightened if you _____ _____ .

5 If I go on Facebook, I might _____ _____ .

6 They won't do it if you _____ _____ .

7 I may not be able to hear, if you _____ _____ .

Language focus extra

be going to / will / Present continuous

1 Match the sentence halves.

1 I'm going to look up _____g_____
2 She won't tell her parents what happened _____
3 Jessica and Bea are starting dance classes tomorrow, _____
4 Where are Harry and Eva going to go _____
5 I'm not going to pay for a new one because _____
6 Noah probably won't join the swimming team _____
7 We're going to write an email to the school, _____
8 I'm playing football with Jacob tomorrow _____

a are you interested?
b I hope they answer.
c it was broken when you gave it to me.
d because they might be angry.
e as he's afraid of water.
f against a team from another school.
g some of these new words in a dictionary.
h on holiday this year?

2 Complete the sentences and questions. Use the verb phrases in the box.

> won't be   won't come   're catching
> 'm not going to do   'm looking after
> 's going to rain   are you going   Is she travelling
> 's getting   're not going   'll be able to spend

1 My cousin_'s getting_ married in June. I'm really excited!
2 They _____ the 8.20 am train, so we _____ all day together.
3 I _____ much this weekend. I'm very tired.
4 We _____ camping this weekend. It _____ for two days.
5 I _____ my little brother this afternoon. I _____ bored!
6 How long _____ on holiday for, Mia?
7 Tom probably _____ to school tomorrow. He's got a hospital appointment.
8 _____ by plane or by train?

Quantifiers

3 Circle the correct options.

1 We haven't got **much** / **many** time. Be quick or we'll be late!
2 Have we got **a few** / **enough** money to get some water?
3 There are **too many** / **any** options. I can't decide which I prefer.
4 They've got **a little** / **a few** nice T-shirts in your size. What about this one?
5 **A lot of** / **Any** people say that it's a nice place, but I haven't been there yet.
6 I think he was angry because I told him I didn't want **any** / **some** help.
7 **How much** / **How many** is it to go on the roller coaster? Is it expensive?
8 They had a pizza because they didn't have **enough** / **a little** time to cook.

4 Complete the sentences with the words in the box.

> enough   How much   few   too many
> too much   ~~some~~   little   lot

1 You took _____some_____ good photos yesterday. Will you send them to me?
2 I had _____ coffee and now I can't sleep.
3 I've got a _____ things to do today. I won't be able to see you.
4 There were _____ people at the concert. I was a bit scared.
5 We've got a _____ orange juice or we've got some water.
6 I don't think we've got _____ money to buy three tickets.
7 _____ pocket money do your parents give you?
8 I have to study a _____ this evening. The exam is tomorrow.

Language focus extra

Second conditional

1 **Match the sentence halves.**

1 If he went to India,
2 It'd be a great idea
3 There would be less pollution
4 If I was a teacher,
5 You wouldn't believe me
6 If he joined the football team,

a if people didn't use their cars every day.
b he'd make lots of friends.
c if we had enough money.
d if I told you.
e he'd visit the Taj Mahal.
f I wouldn't give any homework.

2 **Complete the second conditional sentences. Use the correct form of the verbs in brackets.**

1 If I _____ had _____ (have) enough time, I 'd learn _____ (learn) to play the guitar.
2 She _____ (not be) late for school if she _____ (get up) earlier.
3 If they _____ (know) the answer, they _____ (tell) you.
4 Mr Jones _____ (help) you if you _____ (ask) him nicely.
5 If I _____ (meet) Will Smith, I _____ (ask) for his autograph.
6 Our English _____ (get) better if we _____ (move) to New York.

3 **Complete the sentences using the second conditional.**

1 Mark doesn't study. He gets bad marks. Mark _would get better marks if he studied_ .
2 Ana likes swimming. She goes to the pool every day. If _____ .
3 I'm not going to his house. I don't have time. If _____ .
4 You don't wear your glasses to read. Your eyes hurt. Your _____ .
5 We live in the city. We don't have a horse. If _____ .
6 They aren't on Twitter. I don't follow them. I _____ .

4 **Complete the sentences so they are true for you.**

1 If I liked you, I would …
   buy you a present
2 My bedroom would look nice if …
   _____ .
3 If I had a problem, I would …
   _____ .
4 I would get good marks if …
   _____ .
5 If I grew my hair long, …
   _____ .

Second conditional questions

5 **Complete the questions with the correct form of the verbs in the box.**

| take   go   say   can   ~~have~~   need |

1 If you _____ had _____ a dog, what would you call it?
2 If you didn't feel ill, where _____ you _____ today?
3 What time would we arrive if we _____ the earlier train?
4 If you _____ be a character from a film, who would you be?
5 If he asked you to go out, _____ you _____ yes?
6 Who would you ask if you _____ to borrow some money?

6 **Write second conditional questions with the prompts.**

1 we / share a bedroom / how often / we / argue?
   If we shared a bedroom, how often would we argue?
2 they / like / it / I / stop / speaking to them?
   _____
3 What / his parents / say / they / know?
   _____
4 you / can / have a super power / what / it / be?
   _____
5 you / live in London / the weather / be / better?
   _____
6 you / be / me / what / you / do?
   _____

Language focus extra

Present simple passive

1 **Rewrite the sentences using the present simple passive.**

1 They clean the windows every month.
The _windows are cleaned every month_ .

2 They don't update their blog every day.
The _____ .

3 People take a lot of photos on mobile phones.
A _____ .

4 The hotel serves breakfast from 7–10 am.
Breakfast _____ .

5 They give students a certificate at the end of the year.
Students _____ .

6 People ask a lot of questions in my class.
A _____ .

2 **Use a word from each box to complete the sentences. Use the present simple passive.**

bananas   spaghetti   cakes   ~~tea~~   fish   chocolate

~~drink~~   catch   cook   bake   make   grow

1 ___Tea is drunk___ in most countries.
2 _____ from cocoa beans.
3 _____ in an oven.
4 _____ in rivers and at sea.
5 _____ in the Canary Islands.
6 _____ in boiling water.

Past simple passive

3 **Complete the text with the past simple passive form of the verbs in brackets.**

Modern text messages, or SMS, [1]___were invented___ (invent) in 1992. Early messages [2]_____ (not write) on a mobile phone, they could only be sent from a computer to a phone. The first message in the UK said 'Merry Christmas'. In 1993, the first mobile-to-mobile SMS service [3]_____ (introduce) in Sweden. It wasn't popular immediately, but by 2011, an average of 17.9 billion texts [4]_____ (send) every day. However, technology always moves forward, and in the same year, SMS messages [5]_____ (replace) as the most popular way of sending texts. Chat apps, such as WhatsApp, [6]_____ (use) to send 19 billion texts a day. Experts think this number is going to double in the next two years!

4 **Complete the sentences using the past simple passive and *by*.**

1 The Wright brothers built the first plane.
The first plane _was built by the Wright brothers_ .

2 Alfred Nobel invented dynamite.
Dynamite _____ .

3 Jack Dorsey started Twitter in 2006.
Twitter _____ .

4 A school teacher wrote the song Happy Birthday.
The song Happy Birthday _____
_____ .

5 Walt Disney and Ub Iwerks created Mickey Mouse.
Mickey Mouse _____ .

6 Leonardo da Vinci painted the Mona Lisa.
The Mona Lisa _____ .

Past simple passive questions

5 **Write past simple passive questions with the prompts.**

1 In which language / the first book / print?
In which language was the first book printed?

2 How many hot dogs / eat / by Joey Chestnut in ten minutes?
_____

3 When / basketball / invent?
_____

4 Which language / the English word yoghurt / take / from?
_____

5 How many people / the 2014 World Cup final / watch / by?
_____

6 In what year / the first computer game / release?
_____

6 **Match the answers (a–f) with the questions in Exercise 5.**

a 69   Question: ___
b 1976   Question: ___
c 1 billion   Question: ___
d Turkish   Question: ___
e German   Question: _1_
f 1891   Question: ___

Thanks and acknowledgments

The authors and publishers would like to thank a number of people whose support has proved invaluable during the planning, writing and production process of this course.

We would like to thank Diane Nicholls for researching and writing the Get it Right pages, Alice Martin for writing the original Starter Unit, Ingrid Wisniewska for writing the original Review sections and Mick Green for writing the original Grammar Extra sections.

The authors and publishers are grateful to the following contributors:
Blooberry: concept design
emc design Limited: text design and layout
emc design Limited: cover design
David Morritt and Ian Harker – DSound: audio recordings
Ruth Cox: editing

Development of this publication has made use of the Cambridge English Corpus (CEC). The CEC is a computer database of contemporary spoken and written English, which currently stands at over one billion words. It includes British English, American English and other varieties of English. It also includes the Cambridge Learner Corpus, developed in collaboration with the University of Cambridge ESOL Examinations. Cambridge University Press has built up the CEC to provide evidence about language use that helps to produce better language teaching materials.

The authors and publishers acknowledge the following sources of copyright material and are grateful for the permissions granted. While every effort has been made, it has not always been possible to identify the sources of all the material used, or to trace all copyright holders. If any omissions are brought to our notice, we will be happy to include the appropriate acknowledgements on reprinting.

p. 5 (BL): Corbis/Clifford White; p. 6 (B): Alamy/©Picture Partners; p. 8 (TR): age fotostock/stefano gulmanelli; p. 9 (TR): Getty Images/David Trood; p. 10 (CL): Alamy/©Patrick Eden; p. 11 (BL): Shutterstock Images/Benjamin Simeneta; p. 12 (C): Shutterstock Images/A.Hornung; p. 12 (B): Alamy/©PhotoAlto; p. 15 (BR): Alamy/©MBI; p. 17 (CR): Getty Images/Claudia Dewald; p. 20 (C): Shutterstock Images/Anchiy; p. 21 (BL): Alamy/©Terry Foster; p. 21 (C): Alamy/©My Lit'l Eye; p. 22 (BL): Shutterstock Images/Alexander Raths; p. 25 (TR): Shutterstock Images/lzf; p. 28 (BR): REX/Nils Jorgensen; p. 29 (CR): Alamy/©Roberto Herrett; p. 30 (BR): Alamy/©Scott Hortop Images; p. 31 (BL): Alamy/©Marek Stepan; p. 32 (B): Corbis/Paul Hackett; p. 37 (BR): Alamy/©Cate Brown; p. 38 (TR): Alamy/©Art Directors & TRIP; p. 39 (TL): Shutterstock Images/Monkey Business Images; p. 39 (BR): Shutterstock Images/Mitotico; p. 40 (TL): Shutterstock Images/Roland Zihlmann; p. 41 (TC): Shutterstock Images/ilovezion; p. 41 (TR): Shutterstock Images/Ammit Jack; p. 41 (BL): Shutterstock Images/Anton_Ivanov; p. 42 (CL): Shutterstock Images/NAN728; p. 42 (BL): Getty Images/Rolf Bruderer; p. 47 (TR): Getty Images/Zero Creatives; p. 48 (CL): Shutterstock Images/ARENA Creative; p. 49 (TL): Alamy/©Design Pics Inc.; p. 49 (BR): Getty Images/monkeybusinessimages; p. 50 (BL): Alamy/©Picture Partners; p. 51 (TL): Shutterstock Images/Monkey Business Images; p. 52 (TR): Shutterstock Images/MJTH; p. 54 (CL): Shutterstock Images/wallybird; p. 58 (CR): Alamy/©Westend61 GmbH; p. 60 (TR): Shutterstock Images/Refat; p. 61 (BL): Alamy/©Angela Hampton Picture Library; p. 62 (B): Alamy/©Emiliano Joanes; p. 68 (CL): Alamy/©Jenny Matthews; p. 69 (TL): Shutterstock Images/Olimpik; p. 69 (BR): Shutterstock Images/Photographee.eu; p. 71 (BL): Shutterstock Images/Monkey Business Images; p. 72 (C): Alamy/©imageBROKER; p. 74 (TL): Shutterstock Images/sonya etchison; p. 78 (BL): Alamy/©Jim West; p. 78 (TR): Shutterstock Images/Bakalusha; p. 80 (TR): Alamy/©Islandstock; p. 81 (TL): Shutterstock Images/bikeriderlondon; p. 81 (BL): Alamy/©Michael Klinec; p. 82 (BL): Getty Images/Jupiterimages; p. 84 (TR): Alamy/©Andrew Butterton; p. 88 (B): Alamy/©Caroline Commins; p. 89 (BL): Shutterstock Images/Nagy-Bagoly Arpad; p. 90 (CR): Shutterstock Images/Prudkov; p. 91 (CR): Alamy/©Keith Pritchard/ARGO Images.

Front cover photograph by Getty Images/Eduardo Garcia.

The publishers are grateful to the following illustrators:

David Belmonte p. 19, 27; Russ Cook p. 3 (TL), 35, 65, 75; Nigel Dobbyn p. 14, 57, 77; Mark Draisey p. 7, 59, 68, 70; Mark Duffin p. 9, 29, 79; Andrew Painter p. 18; Martin Sanders p. 3 (R), 55; Tony Wilkins p. 20, 47.

All video stills by kind permission of Discovery Communications, LLC 2015.